Oil Crisis Management

Edward N. Krapels is a consultant
to the U.S. government and the private sector
in matters concerning petroleum management
and policy.

Oil Crisis Management

Strategic Stockpiling for International Security

•

Edward N. Krapels

THE JOHNS HOPKINS UNIVERSITY PRESS

BALTIMORE AND LONDON

This book has been brought to publication with the generous assistance
of The Rockefeller Foundation.

The Johns Hopkins University Press, Baltimore, Maryland 21218
The Johns Hopkins Press Ltd., London

Library of Congress Cataloging in Publication Data

Krapels, Edward N.
  Oil crisis management.

  Includes bibliographical references and index.
  1. Petroleum industry and trade. 2. National security. I. Title.
  HD9560.6.K75   333.8′23217   80-13358
  ISBN 0-8018-2374-9

Contents

●

Tables

Figures

CONTENTS

Foreword

•

A continuous flow of energy is a vital necessity for every modern industrial society. Oil provides most of the energy currently consumed in the industrial countries, and most of that oil comes from members of the Organization of Petroleum Exporting Countries (OPEC). During the 1970s, conflict and political instability in the Middle East resulted in two major oil supply interruptions: one following the Arab-Israeli hostilities in October 1973; the second following the Iranian revolution at the end of 1978. It would be foolish not to anticipate and guard against more interruptions in the 1980s.

One way of enhancing a nation's capability to cope with an oil supply emergency is to amass a reserve stock. Accordingly, each of the major industrial countries has established a petroleum stockpile. There are clear differences, however, in the regulation and administration of national storage programs.

Thus far, the policies and performance of industrial countries regarding emergency petroleum reserves have been neglected areas of energy policy research and analysis. In order to help fill the gap, The Rockefeller Foundation's International Relations Program has supported this pioneer work by Edward N. Krapels. I am very pleased with the results.

Mr. Krapels has collected a wealth of data that is generally inaccessible to those not engaged in the management of petroleum stocks and the development of national and international policies regarding such stocks. He has analyzed this data carefully and in a way that illustrates the connections between petroleum stockpiles and the larger concepts of supply security. And he has compared the policies and plans of the United States with those of France, the German Federal Republic, Japan, Italy, and the Netherlands. He has assessed the prospects for effective international cooperation in future oil supply emergencies through the mechanisms of the International Energy Agency.

This book was completed before the second Iranian crisis of 1979. In November 1979, the United States ceased importing oil from Iran, and was embargoed by Iran in return. Once again, Americans are confronted with the prospect of sudden disruptions in fuel supplies. Once again, the crisis may have to be managed from a position of vulnerability because the American Strategic Petroleum Reserve is so far behind schedule that few emergency supplies are available.

Preliminary indications suggest that—with the possible exception of Japan—governments of oil-importing countries were unable or unwilling to use stocks to manage the Iranian supply loss or to contain the explosive increase in oil prices. There is no doubt that the cessation of Iranian exports early in 1979 would have been far less severe had the United States and other countries been able to draw oil from their strategic reserves in a coordinated manner.

As Mr. Krapels explains, the value of emergency reserves, and consequently the utility of various domestic and international crisis-management plans in the 1980s, is open to question. The principal reason for this clouded security outlook is that strategic reserves are too small. Therefore, governments are reluctant to use them for fear of depleting stock levels for future crises.

Mr. Krapels' work raises disturbing questions about the ability of the industrial countries to cope with future oil disruptions. How much oil is needed in strategic stockpiles? What are the implications of different approaches in the importing countries? Are international crisis-management plans aimed at the kinds of crises that are most likely to occur during the 1980s? To what extent can we rely on the emergency program of the International Energy Agency? Can the importing countries do anything to prevent anarchy in the pricing of international oil supplies?

These are complex issues. This book does not attempt to provide definitive answers. It does, however, offer all of us who are concerned with energy policy a thoughtful and much-needed appraisal of the role of petroleum stocks in managing the oil crises of the 1980s.

                                                          Mason Willrich

Acknowledgments

•

My first of many thank-you's for help in the creation of this book go to Mason Willrich, Director of International Affairs, and Edwin Deagle, Deputy Director of International Affairs, The Rockefeller Foundation. Mason provided the original idea, Ed saw me through the two and a half years of work, and the Foundation provided the fellowship grants.

Most of the research took place while I was a Visiting Research Associate at the Royal Institute for International Affairs in London. Chatham House provided not only its marvelous atmosphere for research but also Mr. Ian Smart, its Director of Studies until 1978, who provided advice and encouragement and expertly chaired the meetings at which the controversial subjects of this book were discussed.

Special thanks are due Mr. Melvin Conant, who gave me the opportunity to get involved in energy security analysis while I was with the Federal Energy Administration. My thanks go as well to Dr. Paul Frankel, in whose footsteps I would follow if I could. More than anyone, he has inspired me to look beyond the technical, on the proviso that it not be disregarded in my search for the political, strategic, and even psychological truths of the oil world.

In gathering information and insights into the oil security policies of the six countries surveyed, I was fortunate to get help from governments and the oil industry. In many cases, the help I got was clearly beyond the call of duty. Fritz Klausner and others of Exxon and its subsidiaries, Enrico Mercanti of Ente Nazionale Idrocarburi, Dr. Franz Bramkamp and his staff at the Ministry of Economics in Bonn, Mr. van Eupen and his staff at the Dutch Ministry of Economics, Philippe Lecourtier and Charles Eyraud of the Direction des Carburants in Paris, Dr. Toyoaki Ikuta of Japan's Institute for Energy, and Dr. Günter Eich of the Commission of the European Communities were especially helpful. Any flaws in the information in this report are my fault, not theirs, and the views expressed herein are my own.

Maureen Dursi was the last and the best of a group of editors who prepared this awkward manuscript for submission to the publisher.

I would also like to acknowledge the special contribution made by Anthony Kooharian, my consultant and my friend. He was the ideal mentor, unsparing of his time, his wit, and his criticism.

Extra special thanks go to Gigi Krapels, who not only contributed to this book but also helped the author as he was trying to write it.

E.N.K.
May 1980

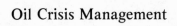

Oil Crisis Management

1

Introduction

•

In November 1978, oil workers in Iran went on strike to protest the rule of the Shah. Production of Iranian crude oil, which had averaged 6 million barrels per day, (b/d), declined to 3.5 million b/d in November, 2.5 million b/d in December, and 500,000 b/d in January 1979.[1] Iran had produced about 10 percent of the total world oil supply; the loss of this oil was the most serious disruption to world energy supplies since the Arab production restrictions of 1973–74. The Iranian oil crisis, like its predecessor, caused dramatic increases in the price of oil in "spot markets" (where individual cargoes are traded), an increase in the price of oil charged by the Organization of Petroleum Exporting Countries (OPEC), and fears of petroleum-product shortages in the countries that depend on OPEC oil imports.

Although these symptoms of an imbalance in the oil market were reminiscent of previous situations, governments of many oil-importing countries held two new cards which they did not have in the Arab oil crisis. Those two cards were (1) the existence of a stand-by international petroleum allocation plan and (2) their own emergency oil stockpiles.

The international oil allocation plan had been drawn up in 1974 by representatives of most of the industrialized oil-importing countries. The plan was part of the International Energy Agreement, which established not only an oil-sharing procedure (commonly referred to as the International Emergency Program, or IEP) but also an administrative body called the International Energy Agency (IEA). The IEA is a forum for energy-related debates among industrial countries, and its Secretariat participates in such diverse activities as research-and-development coordination, multilateral energy-demand forecasting, and energy conservation assessments. Its most valuable contribution during supply emergencies, however, is its capacity to monitor and to some extent

1

direct petroleum shipments to member countries. With the IEA's centralized monitoring and administrative capability, the oil-importing countries now have an option that was not available before, an option to ensure that no member country suffers a substantially larger reduction in oil shipments than any other country.

The second new element that was present when the disruption of Iranian oil production began was the existence of special regulations in all IEA countries governing emergency petroleum reserves. Special stockpiles were being built, or in some countries that had them before 1974, were being maintained specifically to help member countries cope with sudden disruptions in the normal flow of oil supplies. Such stockpiling expresses the principle that it is more sensible to pay to maintain emergency reserves than to expose economies to the need suddenly to reduce the level of oil utilization. Demand for oil is inelastic. Consumers of oil have demonstrated that they will pay much higher prices, in the short run, in order to maintain the level of their oil consumption. If oil prices are not allowed to increase, shortages will be manifested in long lines at gasoline stations, spot shortages of heating oils, and an increase in the number of black markets for oil products.

In principle, an emergency stockpile can mitigate these problems. Oil from the stockpile can be used to replace all or part of the oil lost as a result of the disruption. In practice, however, any oil-stockpiling policy must deal with several complex questions. The most difficult question is how much oil is needed to provide sufficient protection against oil supply disruptions. The answer can be based only on judgments about the probability of future disruptions, their size, and their duration. If oil were cheap and cheap to store, a policy to keep in reserve truly large quantities—say, a two years' supply—might be feasible. But oil is dear and storage facilities are expensive; thus most governments find it difficult to implement such ambitious storage plans. Instead, most have settled for a stockpile that would last less than 90 days, based on the national rate of oil consumption.

National oil stockpiling and multinational oil allocation are the essential elements of international oil security, in the same way that armaments and a good logistics network are essential to military security. Cooperative management of an oil supply crisis would not be feasible if one of the two elements were left out. Emergency supplies are critically important because without them, countries would have to curtail consumption abruptly when normal supplies were disrupted. A multinational allocation program is critically important because without it one country might suffer a much worse oil supply loss than another. If this occurred, the emergency reserves of one country would be depleted much more rapidly than those of other countries.

International Oil Allocation

A fair multinational allocation program and effective national emergency supply policies are obviously important. Less obvious are the definitions of what is fair and what is effective. It is difficult to devise an oil allocation scheme that is unquestionably fair to all the member countries of the IEA. The difficulty stems in the first place from differences in member nations' reliance on oil. The United States, for example, derives only about 50 percent of its energy from oil; the rest comes from natural gas, coal, nuclear power, and hydroelectricity. Japan, in contrast, derives more than 70 percent of its energy from oil. Therefore, a 10 percent oil loss could cause a 5 percent energy loss for the United States, but a 7 percent loss for Japan.

A second factor complicating a fair allocation scheme is the percentage of oil that must be imported. The United States imports 50 percent of its oil, Japan nearly 100 percent. Thus, a 10 percent oil import loss would cause the United States a 5 percent loss in its total oil supplies and a 2.5 percent loss in overall energy. Japan, on the other hand, would lose 10 percent of its total oil supplies and 7 percent, or nearly three times as much, of its overall energy supplies.

Also complicating fair allocation are differences in the efficiency of energy utilization. Some countries require less energy to create a given amount of production or income than others. Therefore, the most efficient countries are likely to lose more production per unit of oil loss than others. Among the industrial countries, comparative studies show that Japan is more efficient than the United States. One study using 1973 data concluded that to produce $1,000 worth of goods and services, Japan used 6.19 barrels of oil, Western Europe used 6.51 barrels, and the United States used 10.18 barrels.[2]

The difficulty of devising a fair multinational allocation program is similar to the problem of devising a fair allocation of oil within one country. During a crisis, farmers, industries, shops, automobile owners, and homeowners compete for supplies from government administrators. The difference between the international and domestic allocation situations is that in the former the contending parties are sovereign nations and participate in the negotiations voluntarily. If things do not go their way, they can abandon the multilateral effort and try to secure a higher level of supplies in the world market. Hence, an international allocation program is inherently fragile; it is only as strong as the willingness of the participants to cooperate voluntarily. The IEP allocation program must be regarded in this context: it will work only as long as its member countries make it work; each member country has the power to hinder its implementation.

The IEP allocation program that emerged in 1974 from the negotiations between member countries is a political compromise. The program, which is described in chapter 3, did not take into account differences in the efficiency of national energy utilization or in the degree of oil dependence. It did take into account differences in the extent of dependence on oil imports.

Emergency Petroleum Reserves

A similar political compromise was struck in negotiations concerning the level of emergency reserves each member should maintain. Government negotiators at the IEA recognized the importance of emergency reserves, and the final IEA agreement requires member countries to acquire by 1980 an "emergency self-sufficiency capability" equivalent to a 90-day supply of net imports.[3] In essence, this stockpiling requirement is one of the prices countries must pay for membership in the IEP.

In theory, an emergency petroleum reserve seems a simple remedy to the oil import security problem. For example, should the United States suddenly lose part of its normal eight million barrels of daily imports, an emergency stockpile properly located and connected to domestic transportation facilities could be deployed to take up the slack. Similarly, stockpiles in Germany, Japan, Turkey, and elsewhere could fill the gap in those nations' imports until the crisis was over. And if every importing country had an emergency reserve of the same minimum size (in proportion, of course, to its oil needs), all could be confident of being able to endure an oil crisis for a similar period of time, a considerable advantage in managing a crisis collectively.

In practice, one level below this simple characterization, a more lively picture emerges. Establishing and maintaining emergency stockpiles raises numerous complex issues, some relating to security questions, others relating to commercial questions. This is an important distinction because while oil security protection is a national security requirement, actually getting the protection in the form of emergency stockpiles can become an important commercial issue that revolves around the question of *who* should establish and maintain emergency reserves.

There are at least two broad options. (1) Oil companies are natural candidates to maintain emergency stocks because they provide, refine, and distribute the oil, functions for which they must maintain substantial oil inventories; but it can be argued (and has been) that it is unfair to place this heavy financial burden on the oil industry. (2) Government can establish and maintain emergency oil stockpiles, using general tax revenues or even a special stockpile tax to pay for this national security good; but this imposes a burden on all taxpayers and could be considered less equitable than the first option, which indirectly imposes the burden on oil consumers.[4]

What is the burden? Primarily it is financial. At a price of $20 to $25 per barrel, a large stockpile of oil is a "dead asset" of considerable proportions. In some countries, oil companies are obliged to keep a stockpile equivalent to the amount of oil they would normally sell in a 90-day period, which ties up a considerable amount of capital. Without the 90-day obligation, most companies would keep a far lower inventory.[5]

The financing issue adds to the complications inherent in an emergency stockpiling program. Strategic issues such as how much oil is needed, what kind of oil should be in stock, and how the oil should be used in a crisis also figure in government planning. These are important security questions, and are complex enough to solve in themselves. However, where the oil industry is obliged to finance the emergency stocks, commercial issues become additional complicating factors. How will the stockpiling be financed? Will all companies (large and small, weak and strong) have the same obligations? Should emergency stocks be segregated from operating inventories?

The commercial issues could be relegated to an appendix in this report if it were clear that they do not affect the security situation. But it is necessary to consider whether commercial issues do affect the security outlook, whether the *manner* in which the oil industry implements government storage obligations affects the size, composition, and availability of emergency stocks for use during a crisis. In short, one must investigate whether the commercial issues affect the quality of the emergency reserve. Moreover, since storage regulations and company modes of implementing them differ in each country, one must consider whether the quality of emergency reserves differs from country to country, and how this would affect international crisis management efforts.

Differences in the quality of national emergency reserves would not be so significant if there were no International Energy Program. However, the IEP represents an international strategy that implicitly relies on its members' emergency reserves.[6] The existence of good and bad stockpiling programs could cause problems in implementing and holding to the IEP crisis management strategy.

Emergency Management Strategies

The objective of emergency management strategies, and of their oil-stockpiling components, is to prevent a reduction in oil imports from damaging the economy of a nation and adversely affecting the life styles of its citizens. It is difficult to go beyond such generalizations to specify how much damage or how great an effect on life styles a government would tolerate.[7] Whatever the answer, the government, and indeed the society, have a limited number of ways to deal with an oil import loss: (1) [increase supplies from foreign producers]; (2) restrain domestic demand; (3) increase domestic production or switch to other fuels; or (4) draw down stocks.[8] The first option is bracketed to indicate that under IEP rules, a country cannot benefit unilaterally by somehow increasing oil shipments from a foreign source; all oil supplies are shared.

The other options all have limits, but importantly, different kinds of limits, to their utility. The level of demand restraint is limited because such restraint causes economic losses after the slack in demand is taken up. There may be some amount of "fat" in national oil-consumption patterns that could be forgone without causing much economic harm, but economies are too complex for analysts to *know* where this "free" demand restraint would end.

Fuel switching and increases in domestic oil production are limited in a more physical sense. The amount of fuel switching that is possible depends on the number of oil users who can switch to coal or gas. The amount by which domestic oil production can be increased is a function of the physical presence of oil and the facilities required to extract it.[9]

Stock drawdowns have yet a different type of limit. One of the advantages of stockpiling is that unlike fuel switching and increases in domestic production, which have a technically based inflexibility, stocks can easily be designed with great drawdown flexibility. On the other hand, fuel switching and the development of domestic production can usually be sustained for several years, while stock drawdowns are a much more transient solution, since each barrel withdrawn brings the stockpile that much closer to depletion.

What is the optimal mix of demand restraint, fuel switching, increases in domestic production, and stock drawdowns? There are two major factors in the answer to this question. The first and most obvious is cost: use the cheapest measure.[10] But this in itself is complicated by the fact that costs will be variable. For example, a 5 percent level of demand restraint may be "free," but 10 percent may cause a 5 percent reduction in the gross national product (GNP), 20 percent may cause a 15 percent reduction in GNP, and so on.[11] These cost profiles will probably differ for each country.

The second factor influencing the optimal mix is the duration of the disruption. A very short disruption (e.g., one of several months) would probably be most efficiently managed by means of stock drawdowns, since demand restraint would be politically unpopular and fuel switching and increases in domestic production would be technically and financially cumbersome (and not available in many countries). At the other extreme, a very long disruption (e.g., one of several years), would probably be managed better by means of demand restraint, fuel switching, and increases in domestic production.

Relying on stock drawdowns in a very long disruption raises the problem of when to stop.[12] If the government could *know* the level and duration of future disruptions, it could devise the optimal mix of crisis management measures. However, although some disruptions have predictable levels and durations (e.g., a rupture in the Alaska pipeline would cause a given level of oil loss, and the duration required for repairs could probably be estimated fairly precisely), there are others whose level and duration cannot be predicted. This is especially true of those caused by political confrontations, in which the duration of the disruption may be perversely related to the level of the emergency reserves of the victim.

This book is an attempt to analyze the oil security outlook of importing countries by examining the two principal components of oil supply defense policies: (1) allocation of oil among importing countries; and (2) the use of emergency petroleum reserves. The chapters that follow provide descriptions and evaluations of the IEP allocation plan (chapters 4 and 5) and of the oil-stockpiling programs of six leading oil-importing countries (chapters 6 and 7). The information and insights gained from these investigations are used to make an integrated assessment of the oil supply security outlook (chapter 8).

An analysis of oil supply security prospects would not be complete, however, without consideration of the context in which the problem exists. The state of the world oil market fundamentally shapes the nature of the oil security problem. For example, the Arab oil curtailments of 1973–74 would not have had their significant impact on world oil trade if the market had not been in a "tight" supply state. The oil security outlook for the 1980s will be influenced by the state of the market, but as will be discussed in chapter 2, the state of the market is difficult to predict.

2

Oil and National
Security

•

History offers numerous instances of a threat to a nation's oil supplies
being taken as a threat to its national security. One of the most dramatic
examples is the American embargo of oil shipments to Japan in 1941,
which has been described by Irvine Anderson, Jr.:

In the final analysis, oil proved to be the critical factor. Unaware of all the
events just recounted [the intricate bureaucratic maneuvers in the American and
British governments and the Standard-Vacuum and Royal Dutch/Shell oil
companies], the Japanese watched actual tanker movements, and from the first
of August [1941] onwards assumed they had been completely cut off from
American oil. They reacted just as most Asian oil experts had predicted for
almost a decade—by deciding to seize the [Netherlands East] Indies [now
Indonesia]. Although events of July 1941 had convinced many Americans that
the Japanese were already committed to a military thrust southwards, this was
not the case. Policy discussions in Tokyo had clearly tended in that direction,
but commitments (or for that matter plans) were seldom discussed that far in
advance, and the [American oil] embargo actually forced a decision that had not
yet been made. With oil reserves for only eighteen months of wartime operations,
the clock began to tick the first of August, and a mounting sense of desperation
permeated Tokyo. As the Japanese perceived the options, they could do nothing
and let their war-making capacity drain away; they could give up their hard-won
gains on the [Chinese] mainland to gain respite from Anglo-American sanctions;
or they could make a final desperate lunge for autonomy. They chose the last
with a plan to protect their flanks by disabling the American fleet at Pearl
Harbor, thrusting south to gain and hold the resources of Southeast Asia, and
gambling on a German victory or a failure of American will. ... It was a reckless
way out of a situation they [the Japanese] themselves had created, but it might
have worked. ... Japan's primary objective on December 7 was the oil of

8

Royal Dutch/Shell and the Standard-Vacuum Oil Company in the Netherlands East Indies. The battleships at Pearl Harbor were destroyed primarily to protect the long tanker route from Sumatra to Honshu.[1]

In today's Japan, the need for oil to fuel military operations is scarcely a problem. The problem is to secure the flow of imported oil to fuel an industrial economy. The impact of oil on Japanese security is now couched in economic rather than military terms, yet the similarities between Japan's degree of dependence on imports in 1939 and its dependence today, and the dissimilarities in the sources of its oil, are striking. In 1939, Japan imported about 90,000 barrels per day, 81 percent of which the United States provided.[2] Today, Japan imports 5 million barrels per day, 80 percent of which is provided by the Organization of Petroleum Exporting Countries.[3] In 1939, Japan lost its normal flow of oil supplies because it antagonized its principal supplier. In 1980, Japan's oil security outlook is more complex. When it relied on one supplier for most of its oil, there were a few threats to its oil supplies that could have a dramatic effect on Japanese security. Now that it relies on a larger number of suppliers, there are more threats to its oil supplies, but they are likely to affect a smaller portion of those supplies.

In the 1980s, the oil supply security of Japan, Western Europe, and the United States will be determined by interactions that are more complex than ever before. The factors affecting the stability of oil imports are not principally military, but political and economic. This more complicated security outlook results from the growing complexity of the world oil supply market. OPEC is a force to be reckoned with, but OPEC is an association of sovereign states, each with its own problems and objectives.

In spite of numerous uncertainties about the oil supply situation in the 1980s, it is possible to carve the overall security problem into categories that can be examined separately. One approach to this analysis is to describe the context in which the security problem exists and the specific types of threats to oil supplies that can be made. With this information, it is possible to evaluate a small number of generic security problems with which governments must contend. The principal elements needed to describe the context, threats, and generic problems are shown in table 1.

The Oil Security Context

The impact that a given disruption in petroleum supplies has on the world market and on importing countries individually is influenced by the structure of the world oil market and by the state of the market at the time of the disruption. The structure of the market is defined by its durable relationships: degree of dependence on oil imports, willingness to export oil at a given price, and the quality of political ties between exporting and importing countries.

The structure and state of the market determine the oil supply security context, but assessing the security implications of any context is a matter of interpretations and judgments. What is a security threat? An oil-importing country's national security is not threatened automatically whenever OPEC countries try to increase the economic or even the political benefits of owning oil resources. As Klaus Knorr has noted, "National security concerns arise [only] when vital national values ... are perceived as being threatened by adverse foreign actions or events. What is regarded as 'vital' is a matter of subjective judgment depending on a nation's hierarchy of values."[4] National security is most clearly threatened by acts of military force against the territory of a country. However, Knorr observes that "there is no reason why economic values and particularly patterns of economic life cannot be regarded as

Table 1
Elements of the Oil Supply Security Problem

Element	Definition
Context	
Structure of the oil market	Who exports oil, who imports oil
State of the oil market	Market shares of OPEC countries
Oil-exporting countries	Economic requirements; political stability; foreign-policy interests
Oil-importing countries	Perceptions of vulnerability; commitment to International Energy Program (IEP)
Threats	
Political disruptions	Embargoes and deliberate reductions in oil production
Internal political turmoil in OPEC country	Disrupted oil production due to revolution
Sudden economic austerity campaign	Oil output level decreased for economic reasons
Terrorism	Damaged oil facilities
OPEC country involved in warfare	Actions against oil facilities
Superpower conflict	Disrupted oil shipping
Generic Problems	
Level of disruption	Amount of oil lost
Duration	Open-ended or limited
Distribution	Who loses oil imports
Price	Spot and long-term price changes

vital. . . . Economic threats are a matter of more or less, and so is threat recognition."[5]

Knorr's observations aptly summarize the difficulty of defining a country's vulnerability to oil supply losses. One barrel less than *consumers* in the United States would *use* at a given price level would be no problem, a million barrels less would perhaps be an inconvenience, but ten million less would undoubtedly cause a major crisis: production of essential goods and services and their distribution to all citizens would be impossible. In short, oil supply losses can cause problems ranging in severity from mere annoyances to grave crises, and although many governments probably believe that the most severe oil losses are also the least likely, the fact that they are within the realm of possibility makes it pertinent for us to examine the context in which they might occur.

STRUCTURE OF THE WORLD OIL MARKET

Only four major industrial countries produce substantial quantities of oil. In decreasing order of production they are the Soviet Union, the United States, Canada, and the United Kingdom. The major oil-exporting countries are clustered around the Middle East and North Africa. Venezuela and Indonesia appear in figure 1 as fringe sources of supply, and are not in fact significant exporters in comparison to some of their oil-rich OPEC fellows in the Middle East. As figure 1 clearly indicates, the principal oil arteries are the sea lanes from the Middle East to Europe, the United States, and Japan.

Although the United States is far less dependent upon Middle Eastern oil for total imports than Europe or Japan, this does not mean that the United States is less vulnerable to disruptions in Mid-East oil supplies. The oil streams coming out of OPEC countries are highly fungible. When the flow of Arab oil to the United States and the Netherlands was disrupted in 1973–74, oil from other OPEC countries filled the vacuum.[6] This fungibility allowed the international oil companies to redirect oil supplies to the United States and the Netherlands by diverting shipments of Iranian, Nigerian, and other oils from Europe and Japan.[7]

More important than who gets oil from whom are the relative market shares of OPEC countries. This factor is important simply because the more concentrated the market, the greater the potential of the leading exporters to cause major disruptions. For example, the United States was an extremely important factor in Japan's oil supply in 1939 because American exports dominated the Pacific market. If Japan had had access to alternative suppliers (aside from the Netherlands East Indies), it could have offset the American embargo by less drastic means.

Table 2 provides figures on world, OPEC, Arab OPEC, and in-

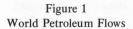

Figure 1
World Petroleum Flows

NOTE: Thickness of the arrows roughly denotes relative proportion of petroleum flows.

dividual OPEC-member oil production levels from 1973 through 1978. The table shows that OPEC's share of world oil production declined from 53.5 percent in 1973 to 48.1 percent in 1978. This decline is principally due to increases in production in the Soviet Union (from 8.6 million b/d in 1973 to 11.5 million b/d in 1978), Mexico (from 524,000 b/d in 1973 to 1.05 million b/d in 1978), and the United Kingdom (from practically none in 1973 to 1.08 million b/d in 1978). However, these increases in non-OPEC production, while undoubtedly important in their respective locales, have not appreciably changed OPEC's vital role in the world market.

Within OPEC, the Arab states' share of world production has remained at about 30 percent. Among the Arab countries, Iraq's market share has gone up to 4.2 percent; Kuwait's and to a lesser extent Libya's have gone down. Saudi Arabia, by far the leading oil-exporting country, has allowed its production and market shares to fluctuate considerably, in keeping with its chosen role as the group's price setter.

Among the other OPEC countries, the most dramatic change is barely reflected in the table. Iran's oil exports plummeted in late 1978 due to strikes by oil workers. At the end of December, oil exports stopped completely and did not resume until March 1979, when they began a slow recovery to 4 million b/d (the level at the time of this writing.)[8]

All in all, table 2 describes a market that is relatively decentralized. Saudi Arabia, the leading exporter, provides only about 13 percent of the world's oil. Of course, the Arab oil exporters as a group command a 30 percent market share, but it is probably less likely that their exports would be disrupted collectively than that the exports of one or several Arab countries would be disrupted during a crisis. Table 2 shows no significant change in market shares from 1973 to 1978. There is no certainty, however, that this pattern will persist during the 1980s. The

Table 2
OPEC's Share of World Oil Production, 1973-78
(in millions of barrels per day)

Oil Production		1973	1974	1975	1976	1977	1978
World	Vol.	57.9	58.0	55.1	59.5	61.7	62.1
	%	100.0	100.0	100.0	100.0	100.0	100.0
OPEC	Vol.	31.0	30.7	27.2	30.8	31.4	29.9
	%	53.5	52.9	49.4	51.8	50.9	48.1
Arab OPEC	Vol.	17.9	17.6	16.0	18.5	19.3	18.5
	%	30.9	30.3	29.0	31.1	31.3	29.8
Saudi Arabia	Vol.	7.6	8.5	7.1	8.6	9.2	8.3
	%	13.1	14.7	12.9	14.5	14.9	13.4
Kuwait	Vol.	3.0	2.5	2.1	2.2	2.0	2.1
	%	5.2	4.3	3.8	3.7	3.2	3.4
Abu Dhabi	Vol.	1.3	1.4	1.4	1.6	1.7	1.4
	%	2.2	2.4	2.5	2.7	2.8	2.2
Iraq	Vol.	2.0	1.9	2.2	2.4	2.5	2.6
	%	3.4	3.3	4.0	4.0	4.1	4.2
Libya	Vol.	2.2	1.5	1.5	1.9	2.1	2.0
	%	3.8	2.6	2.7	3.2	3.4	3.2
Algeria	Vol.	1.1	1.0	0.9	1.1	1.1	1.2
	%	1.9	1.7	1.6	1.8	1.8	1.9
Iran	Vol.	5.9	6.1	5.4	5.9	5.7	5.2
	%	10.2	10.5	9.8	9.9	9.2	8.4
Nigeria	Vol.	2.1	2.3	1.8	2.1	2.1	1.9
	%	3.6	4.0	3.3	3.5	3.4	3.1
Venezuela	Vol.	3.4	3.0	2.3	2.3	2.2	2.2
	%	5.9	5.2	4.2	3.9	3.6	3.5
Indonesia	Vol.	1.3	1.4	1.3	1.5	1.7	1.6
	%	2.2	2.4	2.4	2.5	2.8	2.6

Source: *Petroleum Economist* 46 (April 1979): 177.

amount of oil OPEC will be "asked" to supply to meet world demand for imports depends in part on OPEC itself: the oil prices OPEC sets will influence the economic growth of its customers. Moreover, individual OPEC countries may disregard their customers and establish production ceilings for domestic reasons that will effectively create a shortage. Naturally, this shortage will be reflected in higher prices in the world oil market, unless importing countries somehow manage to control the process whereby oil firms bid up the price of oil.[9]

STATE OF THE WORLD OIL MARKET IN THE 1980S

The uncertainties about OPEC oil pricing and the world economic growth rate make determining the future state of the world oil market a very tenuous business. Each year since 1973, economists have provided new forecasts, most of which have lost their credibility quickly.[10] In 1978, four of the most publicized forecasts were issued by Exxon, the U.S. Department of Energy, the International Energy Agency, and the Petroleum Industry Research Foundation of New York. Their forecasts of demand for OPEC oil in 1985 are shown in table 3.

The estimates in table 3 can be interpreted as follows: the best recent estimates of qualified oil analysts are that demand for OPEC oil in 1985 will be between 32.8 million b/d and 48.7 million b/d. Where within this wide range actual demand for OPEC oil will fall depends on the economic growth rate of industrial countries, which is influenced by the price of OPEC oil, which is influenced in turn by the amount of oil OPEC decides to export. OPEC's total production in 1978 was 29.9

Table 3
Forecasts of the Demand for OPEC Oil in 1985

Source	Assumed OECD Annual Economic Growth Rate	Demand for OPEC Oil (in millions of b/d)	Source	Assumed OECD Annual Economic Growth Rate	Demand for OPEC Oil (in millions of b/d)
DOE	4.6	48.7	EXXON	3.8	40.0
DOE	4.1	44.6	EXXON	3.3	34.0
DOE	3.6	35.0	PIRINC	4.3	41.1
IEA[a]	4.3	48.0	PIRINC[b]	3.8-4.3	36.6
IEA[a]	4.3	42.0	PIRINC	3.8	32.8
EXXON	4.3	46.0			

Source: U.S., State Department Bureau of Intelligence and Research, "Analytical Survey of Recent World Energy Forecasts," Report no. 1110, January 3, 1979.
[a] Basis for variation not specified.
[b] Lower growth rate with high energy coefficient and higher growth rate with low energy coefficient produce the same results.

million b/d, of which 1.3 million b/d were used in OPEC countries. Thus, OPEC output would have to increase by a minimum of 4.2 million b/d and a maximum of 20.1 million b/d to satisfy projected demand.

The OPEC supply outlook is riddled with equally fundamental mysteries. Experts generally try to predict the oil production capacity that OPEC members *could* attain by 1985 and 1990. Whether each country will take the steps necessary to attain these production capacities is a separate problem, as is the question of whether the governments of these countries would choose to produce at or near those capacities even if they were attained. In the face of these unknowns, OPEC supply forecasts must be taken with an even larger dose of salt than world demand forecasts. Thus, the OPEC supply estimates shown in table 4 should be viewed with caution.

A U.S. Central Intelligence Agency (CIA) analysis of the OPEC supply outlook casts Saudi Arabia in the role of the "swing" producer. The report notes that "the Saudis have the reserves needed to support production at this level [i.e., up to 20 million b/d]."[11] The agency also observes pessimistically Saudi Arabia's willingness to establish such a high production capacity:

We doubt that an expansion of this magnitude could be completed by 1985 without a major shift in Saudi priorities. Riyadh is committed to ambitious industrialization programs which are stretching management and logistical capabilities extremely thin ... Even with adequate capacity, the Saudis might well be reluctant to produce at the rates required. ... Should Saudi Arabia allow production to reach 20 million barrels per day by the mid-1980's, output would begin to decline in the 1990's because of reserve depletion. Raising

Table 4
Forecasts of OPEC Production Capacity in 1985
(in millions of barrels per day)

Source	Amount
U.S. Department of Energy	36.8–38.8
International Energy Agency	36.0–38.0
U.S. Central Intelligence Agency	
OPEC, excluding Saudi Arabia	27.5–29.5
Saudi Arabian production required if world demand for oil is:	
32.8 million b/d	3.4–5.3
48.7 million b/d	19.3–21.2

Sources: For the DOE and IEA, same as table 3. For the CIA, U.S. Central Intelligence Agency, *The International Energy Situation: Outlook to 1985* (Washington, D.C.: Government Printing Office, April 1977), pp. 15–17.

production to that level, moreover, could not be accomplished without flaring large quantities of [natural] gas, which the Saudis are determined to avoid.[12]

The CIA'a assessment identifies one of the key problems from the standpoint of security analysis: Are Saudi Arabia and the other principal oil exporters being encouraged by the actions of the oil importers to adopt policies that will lead to an adequate flow of oil to importing countries? This raises a broader security question: Are there forces outside the control of oil importers that will tend to destabilize the oil policies of OPEC countries?

THE OIL-EXPORTING COUNTRIES

The preceding discussion indicates the difficulty of predicting with confidence the state of the world oil market in the 1980s. Some forecasts indicate that demand for OPEC oil will evolve so that Saudi Arabia will be asked to produce up to 20 million b/d by 1985. An important ramification of a market in which the Saudis produce that much oil is that it provides Riyadh with an even greater potential to disrupt the market, whether the disruption is caused by a deliberate act of the Saudi government or by its enemies.

The stability of the world oil market clearly depends upon the internal stability of OPEC states, the relations between OPEC states, and the relations between importing nations and OPEC states. Immediately after the 1973-74 embargo, most oil security analysts were justifiably concerned about the probabilities of future embargoes. More recently, a number of experts have warned that oil supply and price security may be affected most of all by the post-1973 *economic* development within OPEC countries.[13]

Walter Levy has noted that an examination of internal economic situations reveals that

Sooner or later many [OPEC] producing countries will seriously question the value of much of their development program in terms of its potential contribution to their economic progress, political stability, employment, budgetary receipts, and foreign exchange income. Many of them will painfully realize that their industrial efforts could not possibly begin to replace the government and foreign exchange revenues that they have become accustomed to receiving from their oil production, nor provide them with a prosperous non-oil based economy.[14]

Levy argues that all the OPEC countries

[have] to cope with the political and social problems that have been posed by this vast inflow of money: the feverish rate of development; the negative impact on agriculture and traditional industries; their increasing dependence on subsidies for imports; the unhealthy urbanization; the excesses of a building boom; the large influx of foreign labor; inflation; the lopsided distribution of wealth; and

many other politically and socially destabilizing factors. They will realize that rapid and forced development tends to weaken, if not destroy, established social and cultural values. ... Sooner or later there may be a wave of disappointment, frustration, and resentment, most likely directed largely against the foreigner and the producing countries' national governments and their institutions. The [1979] turmoil in Iran is indicative of what may be ahead.[15]

The conclusion of Levy's analysis, though by no means accepted by all oil experts, is that the principal threat to a stable flow of oil supplies in the 1980s may not be conflicts between individual OPEC states and importing countries; nor will it be conflicts among OPEC states. Rather, major disruptions may stem from developments within the OPEC states themselves.

THE OIL-IMPORTING COUNTRIES[16]

On November 21, 1973, Secretary of State Kissinger warned the Arab nations that "the United States would consider counter-measures if the oil embargo is continued indefinitely or unreasonably."[17] This remark, made when the duration and severity of the Arab oil curtailments were unknown and frightening factors, implied that there was a breaking point in the American economy's short-term ability and willingness to adjust to an oil loss. Kissinger did not state where that point might lie, but in January 1975 he partially clarified his comment:

Some of my remarks have created a certain hysteria ... about the possible use of force by the United States. ... It is important to understand what I said: ... in case of actual strangulation of the industrialized world, we would reserve our position. Now, if you analyzed this, no Secretary of State could say less. We cannot take the position that no matter what the producing countries do, we will acquiesce.[18]

Nevertheless, even hinting at the possibility of using armed force to secure oil supplies poses in a fundamental way the question of the relationship between energy and security. At what point do oil shortages create sufficient problems to justify armed retaliation?

There are only rough guesses, no detailed and systematic analyses, of the ability of industrial economies to adjust to oil losses in the short term. For example, in early 1975 the U.S. Treasury Secretary submitted to President Ford an assessment of the relationship between dependence on oil imports and national security:

Any sudden disruption in excess [of 1 million b/d] would have a prompt substantial effect upon our economic well-being, and, considering the close relation between this nation's economic welfare and our national security, would clearly threaten to impair our national security. Furthermore, [in the event of a complete loss' of oil imports] the total U.S. production of about 11 million barrels per day[19] might well be insufficient to supply adequately a war-time economy. As a result, the national security would not merely be threatened, but could be immediately, directly and adversely affected.[20]

In the same report, the Department of Defense stated: "The degree of our energy self-sufficiency must be such that any potential supply denial will be sustainable for an extended period without degradation of military readiness or operations, and without significant impact on industrial output or the welfare of the populace."[21]

The Treasury's estimates are similar to those previously presented in the *Project Independence Report* of the Federal Energy Administration.[22] The report states that if supplies were lost for one year, the first million barrels of daily oil supplies forgone (about 6 percent of total oil supplies) would not result in significant economic losses. The second million barrels lost would result in an economic (GNP) loss of about $30 billion (less than 3 percent of the GNP). Additional losses of oil would result in increasing economic losses; that is, the ratio of economic loss to oil loss would increase. According to this estimate, a total loss of American oil imports for one year would result in a GNP loss of more than $150 billion in the crisis year, which would dribble on, with decreasing force, in subsequent years. This, of course, would be an economic disaster of 1930s proportions.

These estimates, however, do not explicitly account for the manner in which energy consumers, with appropriate government encouragement, might prevent or minimize economic losses. They are derived in a fashion that may overstate in particular the costs of the initial oil losses, and thereby leave an impression of extreme sensitivity. Other observers have made generous estimates of the ability of industrial countries to adjust to oil supply disruptions. Cooper, for instance, has said that short-term adaptability is "surprisingly great,"[23] although he does not give evidence to support his opinion. More significantly, the experience of the United States in World War II suggests that an industrial economy can digest a big energy loss and still achieve a healthy growth rate, if the "necessary measures" are made known to and accepted by the populace.[24]

National vulnerability to oil supply losses has not only a technical dimension, the amount the consumer can save without reducing his economic contribution to the society, but also the dimension of the consumer's willingness to make such an effort, which depends on the political circumstances surrounding the oil loss. The technical dimension is immensely complicated and varies from country to country and regionally within most countries as well. It is compounded by uncertainties about public reaction to oil losses, and that reaction is influenced by attitudes toward the issue responsible for the loss and toward the government, the time of year (a winter shortage would be physically more uncomfortable than a summer one), and the overall health of the economy. According to one analysis, "A threat to economic security is not only a function of the magnitude of an external economic influence, but also of the strength of the socio-political systems which are confronted by such a challenge."[25]

Threats to Oil Supplies

It is evident that future oil supply prospects are uncertain. The level of demand for OPEC oil, the level of production OPEC will be willing to provide, and the price of OPEC oil are unknown. It is unclear whether Saudi Arabia will increase its production to 15–20 million b/d, and whether the disenchantment Walter Levy has warned of could produce a sudden reduction in output. It is also difficult to determine what level of oil supply reduction importing countries could tolerate.

In the face of these uncertainties, only the overall conditions that define the possible states of the oil market in the 1980s can be indicated. Threats to security of supply can be examined in the context of these conditions to unearth somewhat systematic indications of the potential severity of the security problem. Two basic sets of market conditions can exist in the 1980s: a "loose market," in which OPEC's production capacity *and* desired production level substantially exceed world demand for OPEC oil; and a "tight market," in which OPEC's production capacity and desired production level do not substantially exceed world demand for OPEC oil.

Loose market conditions prevailed throughout the 1960s, when the United States was producing as much as 4 million b/d below capacity and the production capacity increases in Saudi Arabia, Libya, and other OPEC countries outpaced the growth in demand for OPEC oil. By the early 1970s, this surplus capacity had been drained by the sharply rising demand for oil. As a result, the late-1973 production cuts by Arab countries could not be offset by production increases elsewhere. The loose market reappeared, however, in 1975 and lasted until early 1978 as demand for OPEC oil relaxed in reaction to the sharp OPEC oil price increases of 1973.

The cessation of Iranian oil exports in late 1978, coupled with the decision by Saudi Arabia and other countries with spare production not to offset the loss completely, reintroduced tight market conditions. Many experts fear that the tight market—a somewhat artificial one, since sufficient *capacity* exists to satisfy demand at the prevailing price—will continue into the 1980s. This outlook is based on declarations from OPEC's leading producers that they intend to continue to restrict production for the time being. Iran's new government has repeatedly stated that it will limit production to 4 million b/d, as compared to 6 million b/d before the revolution. In March 1979, Saudi Arabia reimposed a production ceiling of 8.5 million b/d after allowing a ceiling of 9.5 million b/d to offset the loss of Iranian oil. As a result, oil prices in early 1979 jumped, spot-market transactions zoomed to over $20 per barrel, and OPEC countries responded by imposing not only a 10 percent increase in their posted price but also "temporary" surcharges of up to 10 percent. [26]

It is possible, of course, that the tight market that prevailed in the spring of 1979 will give way to a loose market in the 1980s. Effective conservation measures by importing countries, increased production by OPEC countries, and the emergence of new oil exporters such as Mexico could induce this transition. For security-planning purposes, therefore, the prospects of disruptions to both tight and loose markets must be examined.

The history of the world petroleum market presents six categories of supply disruptions:

1. *Political disruptions—deliberate export restrictions imposed to influence foreign events.* There have been four such incidents: the Arab oil embargoes of 1973–74, 1967, 1957, and 1946. All were connected with Arab-Israeli conflicts.

2. *Production disruptions due to internal unrest in OPEC countries.* Two incidents had the most significant impact on the world oil market: the Iranian revolution of 1978–79 and the Nigerian Civil War of 1967–70.

3. *Sudden supply reductions for domestic economic reasons.* After the large oil price increases of 1973, a number of OPEC states reduced exports in order to prolong the life span of their oil resources. Prominent among them were Libya (from 2.2 million b/d in 1973 to 1.5 million b/d in 1975) and Kuwait (from 3 million b/d in 1973 to 2 million b/d in 1975).

4. *Terrorist acts or sabotage against oil or oil-related installations.* So far, there has been little terrorist action against OPEC facilities. In the Arab world, this is no doubt due to the careful cultivation of good relations with the Palestine Liberation Organization.

5. *War involving OPEC states.* OPEC states have not been involved in a major war since Algeria's war for independence in the early 1960s. However, several OPEC states are involved in long-standing disputes with neighboring states: Iraq and Kuwait have quarreled over a boundary demarcation; Libya and Egypt have had border skirmishes.

6. *Shipping disruptions due to superpower conflicts.* The Soviet Union is capable of threatening oil supply lanes.

Each type of disruption can be characterized in terms of three principal dimensions: the size of the net reduction in world oil supplies, the duration of the disruption, and the distribution of remaining oil supplies among importing countries.

Contingency oil supply planners in importing countries must assess a reduction in world supplies in terms of the amount of spare production capacity that is available in countries not involved in the disruption, and the willingness of those governments to bring spare capacity into production. The Arab oil restrictions of 1967 and the losses caused by the Nigerian Civil War of 1967-70 were offset by increased production elsewhere. However, the loss of Iranian oil in late 1978 was only partially offset by increased output in Saudi Arabia and other OPEC countries. In general, one of the principal reasons why the supply disruptions of the 1970s were regarded as crises and those of the 1960s were not is that by the early 1970s spare production capacity in the United States had disappeared. In 1965 it was nearly 3 million b/d, in 1969 it was 2 million b/d, and in 1973 it was practically gone.[27]

Unlike the level of oil supply loss, the duration of the loss is often impossible to calculate. This is especially true for deliberate, politically motivated export curtailments such as the 1973-74 Arab oil embargo. From a planning standpoint, such disruptions may have to be assumed to be "open-ended." Production restrictions implemented for domestic economic reasons, as in Kuwait and Libya in 1974, also should be viewed as "open-ended." In such cases, the task of emergency programs is to help the economy adjust to a permanently lower level of oil use.[28] In contrast, oil supply disruptions due to civil unrest, acts of terrorism, or warfare should be seen as having a limited duration, because in these instances it is likely that production will be resumed as soon as facilities can be repaired.

In addition to level and duration, oil supply disruptions can be characterized in terms of two types of distribution: targeted or untargeted. The Arab oil disruption of 1967 was aimed at the United Kingdom and the United States. The embargo of 1973-74 was aimed at the United States and the Netherlands. However, such embargoes were thwarted by the ability of the international oil companies to redirect oil shipments so that available supplies were distributed fairly evenly. Other types of disruptions tend not to be targeted against individual importers. Even though, for example, the United States is the principal importer of Nigerian crude, a disruption in exports from that country would be unlikely to be transmitted directly, because the international oil companies could divert other supplies to the United States.[29] The major oil companies' control over the distribution of unaffected oil supplies will be a prime factor in the success of the International Energy Program.

Considering the general characteristics of oil supply disruptions and the types of disruptions described above in the context of loose or tight market conditions invokes several preliminary insights about oil security prospects for the 1980s.

First, if a loose market prevails—that is, if there is some spare production capacity—supply disruptions can be offset by increased production elsewhere. Whether the governments that control such spare capacity will bring it into production is another question; but the capacity exists, and thus, so does the possibility that governments can be persuaded to use it. Disruptions not associated with a conflict between producers and consumers are most likely to be offset by calling up spare production. In a loose market, a deliberate reduction imposed in pursuit of a foreign-policy objective—e.g., another Arab embargo—may have to be maintained for a considerable period of time if non-Arab producers increase their production. The duration of a deliberate embargo thus may be affected by market conditions. Finally, in a loose market it is more difficult for disrupting states to control the distribution of supplies. The availability of spare capacity facilitates oil industry efforts to redirect oil shipments to embargoed countries.

A tight market confronts importing countries with a completely different security outlook. The unavailability of spare production capacity means that any type of disruption will cause an oil loss that is irreplaceable in the short run. Hence, the duration of a disruption that would cause problems for importing countries is shortened. Moreover, since all available supplies are committed before a disruption begins, it is more difficult to redirect supplies fairly to all countries. As in the loose market, a deliberate embargo is most threatening, but it is even more difficult for importing countries to manage under tight market conditions.

The validity of these observations can be examined by reviewing the development of the 1973–74 Arab oil crisis. It occurred in a tight market, its duration was uncertain, and it cut off shipments of Arab oil to the United States and the Netherlands.

3

The 1973–74
Oil Crisis

•

The importing countries' problems during the 1973–74 crisis can be described as follows. Under the spell of uncertainty about the level and duration of the producers' supply restrictions and about the manner in which world oil supplies would be allocated by the international oil companies, the oil-importing governments faced a set of interconnected decisions on how to minimize the impact of the crisis on their economies. Broadly speaking, they could (1) restrain domestic oil demand by letting petroleum-product prices rise or by restricting the quantities put on the market; (2) use oil from stockpiles to replace the lost imports; and (3) compete with other countries to obtain more oil supplies.

In this chapter, the differences in the management responses of selected governments to the oil crisis will be examined briefly, with particular attention being paid to stock drawdowns. It is apparent that economies are not machines with control dials corresponding to the management options noted above. They are complex systems, and the statistics depicting oil supply and pricing developments during the crisis provide only rough indications of the effects of various types of government programs.

The Level and Duration of Supply Restrictions and the Distribution of Supplies

The 1973–74 oil crisis resulted from the dissatisfaction of some Arab oil producers with the position of some countries, most notably the United States, on Israel's occupation of territories formerly held by Egypt,

Syria, and Jordan. Arab governments reduced oil production near the end of October 1973 and embargoed the shipment of their oil to, among others, the United States and the Netherlands. The Arab states restricted oil output from October 1973 until March 1974, when full production was restored and the embargo on the United States was lifted. [1] The monthly production levels of all the OPEC countries from September 1973 until April 1974 are shown in table 5.

The table illustrates that Saudi Arabia, Kuwait, and Libya made the largest initial cuts. In January, they all increased production, but then Iraq, which had not cut production significantly before, reduced its exports by 300,000 b/d. In March, the collective disruption was called off, and by April, production in Saudi Arabia and the United Arab Emirates had surpassed the levels of September 1973. Kuwaiti and Libyan production, on the other hand, remained below the September level, not as part of an embargo strategy, but because the price increases of December 1973 provided ample revenues at lower output levels.

Table 5 also shows that although non-Arab countries did not participate in the restrictions, they did not or could not increase production

Table 5

OPEC Oil Production, September 1973–April 1974

(in millions of barrels per day)

Oil Production	Sep.	Oct.	Nov.	Dec.	Jan.	Feb.	Mar.	Apr.
Arab Countries								
Saudi Arabia	8.5	7.8	6.3	6.6	7.5	7.8	8.1	8.7
Kuwait	3.5	3.1	2.6	2.6	2.8	2.8	2.8	2.8
UAE	1.4	1.3	1.2	1.0	1.2	1.3	1.5	1.6
Qatar	0.6	0.6	0.5	0.5	0.5	0.5	0.5	0.5
Libya	2.3	2.4	1.8	1.8	2.0	1.9	1.9	1.7
Iraq	2.2	1.8	2.0	2.1	1.8	1.8	1.8	1.9
Algeria	1.1	1.0	0.9	0.9	1.0	1.0	1.0	1.0
Total	19.6	18.0	15.3	15.5	16.8	17.1	17.6	18.2
Non-Arab Countries								
Iran	5.8	6.0	6.0	6.1	6.1	6.2	6.1	6.2
Nigeria	2.1	2.2	2.2	2.3	2.2	2.2	2.3	2.3
Venezuela	3.4	3.4	3.4	3.3	3.3	3.2	3.2	3.0
Indonesia	1.4	1.4	1.4	1.4	1.5	1.4	1.4	1.4
Ecuador	0.2	0.2	0.2	0.2	0.2	0.2	0.2	0.2
Gabon	0.2	0.2	0.2	0.2	0.2	0.2	0.2	0.2
Total	13.1	13.4	13.4	13.5	13.5	13.4	13.4	13.3
Total for OPEC Countries	32.7	31.4	28.7	29.0	30.3	30.5	31.0	31.5
World Production	57.5	56.0	53.1	53.7	55.5	55.7	56.3	56.9

Source: *Oil and Gas Journal*, October 1973–May 1974.

substantially to replace the Arab oil. From September to November, their combined production level increased by only 300,000 b/d, as opposed to a reduction in Arab supplies of 4.3 million b/d. This shows that the oil market in the fall of 1973 was tight—that there was little spare production capacity available, a fact which gave the Arab producers close control over the level of supply reductions experienced by the importing countries collectively. The level of oil losses experienced by individual importers, however, could not be fixed by the producers. Nor could an importing country determine its import level, because the international oil companies, principally the seven "majors,"[2] controlled the distribution of oil. An analysis of the behavior of American oil companies during the crisis showed that while the Arab governments' order to embargo Arab oil shipments to the United States and the Netherlands was obeyed, the companies were able to use their non-Arab oil supplies "to blunt the edge of the Arab oil weapon by redistributing global supplies so that the constriction of supplies was fairly evenly allocated."[3]

The supply curtailments put the oil companies in a difficult position. An Exxon executive explained his company's response to the situation before a U.S. congressional committee: "We did three things. One, we complied with all of the producing countries' embargoes as they ordered and we had no alternative because otherwise the consequences would have been much more severe. ... Second, we respected all of our contractual obligations in the world, using *force majeure* equitable reductions. ... Then, finally, we distributed the crude oil to our affiliated companies on as equitable a basis as we could."[4] He concluded by stating his opinion that "this is a job that ... should have been done by Government and Government failed to do it."[5]

Table 6 compares the level of crude-oil imports of the countries surveyed in this book from October 1973 to March 1974 with the level of imports from October 1972 to March 1973. The import indexes reflect the combined effects of the exporters' embargo, the allocation by the oil companies, and the efforts by some governments to secure additional imports. The data indicate that the United States, Japan, France, and Italy were successful in increasing the amount of crude imports during the crisis, compared with the same period the year before, whereas Germany and the Netherlands were not successful. By presenting only crude-oil data, however, the table fails to show the differences in these countries' imports and exports of finished products.[6]

Table 7 makes the same comparisons between the crisis months and the year before, but presents the differences in *net* oil imports; that is, it adds crude and product imports and deducts crude and product exports. This table shows that the differences among the European

Table 6

Index and Totals of Crude-Oil Imports for Selected Countries, October 1972-March 1973 and October 1973-March 1974

(October = 100)

Country	Year	Oct.	Nov.	Dec.	Jan.	Feb.	Mar.	Oct.-Mar. Average Imports (in thousands of b/d)	% Difference, 1973-74/ 1972-73
U.S.A.	1972-73	100	92	108	108	116	128	2,708	
	1973-74	100	95	78	65	59	68	2,875	+6.2
Japan	1972-73	100	99	108	108	95	100	4,656	
	1973-74	100	93	100	95	84	100	5,001	+7.4
Germany	1972-73	100	114	109	112	113	114	2,149	
	1973-74	100	96	88	87	80	84	2,099	−2.3
France	1972-73	100	120	104	122	114	124	2,696	
	1973-74	100	109	91	96	105	90	2,744	+1.8
Italy	1972-73	100	105	100	93	99	105	2,481	
	1973-74	100	95	101	103	102	97	2,531	+2.0
Netherlands	1972-73	100	100	87	100	104	96	1,456	
	1973-74	100	103	53	81	80	85	1,272	−12.6

Sources: U.S. Bureau of Mines, *Monthly Petroleum Statements*; Petroleum Association of Japan; Commission of the European Communities, *Report by the Commission on the Behaviour of the Oil Companies in the Community during the Period from October 1973 to March 1974* (Brussels: European Economic Community, December 1976), p. 59.

countries in crude imports were reduced by countertrends in product trade. Specifically: (1) the Netherlands increased average product imports (by only 1,000 b/d) and decreased average product exports (by 141,000 b/d); (2) France decreased product imports (by 53,000 b/d) and increased product exports (by 7,000 b/d); and (3) Italy decreased product imports (by 40,000 b/d) and increased product exports (by 4,000 b/d).

Table 7 also shows considerable differences between the United States and Japan on the one hand and the European countries on the other. The differences may be due to decisions by the oil companies to take pre-embargo growth rates into account in allocating oil supplies. In the period 1969-1973 the average oil import growth rates were:[7]

United States	18.8%	France	11.9%
Japan	11.3%	Italy	7.3%
Germany	7.7%	Netherlands	6.3%

Demand Restraint Responses

The level of net imports does not reflect the impact of a crisis on consumers, however, because petroleum stocks can augment oil imports. Table 8 shows the monthly evolution of the sales of principal finished products to consumers in the six countries during the 1973-74 crisis.

Tables 6 and 7 portray what the governments of the importing countries had to contend with regarding crude imports and net imports, respectively. Table 9 indicates roughly what happened to oil consumption within each importing country as a result of government responses to

Table 7

Comparison of the Level of Net Imports in the Periods October 1972–March 1973 and October 1973–March 1974

(in thousands of barrels per day)

Net Imports	U.S.A.	Japan	Germany	France	Italy	Netherlands
Oct. 1972–Mar. 1973	5,287	4,783	2,743	2,621	2,067	760
Oct. 1973–Mar. 1974	5,449	5,033	2,666	2,608	2,073	718
Percentage Difference in Net Imports 1973-74/1972-73	+3.1	+5.2	−2.8	−0.5	+0.3	−5.5
compared with						
Percentage Difference in Crude Imports	+6.2	+7.4	−2.3	+1.8	+2.0	−12.6

Sources: Same as for table 6.

the import situation. Together, the tables indicate substantial differences in the situations faced by the importing countries and in the nature of their responses (table 9).

The comparison indicates that Germany and the Netherlands "lost" the most imports and restrained consumption most vigorously. France and Japan neither lost imports nor lowered consumption. Italy was unique in increasing imports and lowering consumption. The United States increased its crude imports, but lowered its product imports and lowered consumption.

An important factor influencing domestic sales and consumption was the price of oil products in the market. In the United States, the oil companies were allowed to pass on the increased cost of crude-oil imports (not domestic crude, whose price level was controlled by the government) to their customers.[8] In the European Economic Community (EEC), the prices companies could charge for finished products, and therefore the return they could get for the higher crude prices they had to pay for

Table 8

Index of Changes in Domestic Oil Sales, October 1972–March 1973
and October 1973–March 1974

(October = 100)

Country	Year	Oct.	Nov.	Dec.	Jan.	Feb.	Mar.	Total Sales (mm bbls)	% Change
U.S.A.[a]	1972–73	100	107	114	113	115	104	3,292	
	1973–74	100	107	102	100	101	94	3,135	−4.8
Japan[b]	1972–73	100	113	127	115	127	125	765	
	1973–74	100	108	112	101	112	107	818	+6.9
Germany	1972–73	100	106	110	114	113	107	503	
	1973–74	100	97	84	86	66	73	456	−9.3
France	1972–73	100	111	122	130	128	120	452	
	1973–74	100	104	111	102	96	91	456	+0.9
Italy[c]	1972–73	100	103	115	108	113	104	321	
	1973–74	100	96	105	109	109	98	302	−5.9
Netherlands	1972–73	100	113	110	113	114	105	102	
	1973–74	100	85	85	79	88	74	93	−8.8

Source: U.S. Central Intelligence Agency, *International Oil Developments*, Statistical Survey, October 21, 1976, pp. 16–18.

[a] Including marine bunkers, refinery fuel, and losses.
[b] Excluding crude oil burned directly and liquified petroleum gas.
[c] Principal products only.

Table 9
Comparison of Changes in Crude Imports, Net Imports, and Domestic Sales,
October 1972-March 1973 and October 1973-March 1974
(percentage change)

Imports and Sales	U.S.A.	Japan	Germany	France	Italy	Nether-lands
Crude-Oil Imports	+6.2	+7.4	−2.3	+1.8	+2.0	−12.6
Net Imports (Crude and Products)	+3.1	+5.2	−2.8	−0.5	+0.3	−5.5
Domestic Sales	−4.8	+6.9	−9.3	+0.9	−5.9	−8.8

OPEC oil, varied from country to country. The European Commission's investigation of the crisis noted the "extreme difference between the prices practised in the countries of the [EEC] Community. This necessarily distorted competition, although it is impossible over the short period of the crisis to assess the real effect of this on production and trade."[9] In the Netherlands, France, and Italy, the retail prices of most petroleum products were fixed by the government, a move which checked the rise in the prices that would have occurred, but which as an EEC report noted, "inject[ed] a degree of unreality into the market for oil products in these countries."[10] Prices were not controlled in Germany, "the only market [in the EEC in] ... which a large number of suppliers actively competed with each other."[11]

The difference in price regimes is evident in table 10, which lists the prices in the EEC as of April 30, 1974. Although the crisis had ended, Germany's prices were still uniformly higher, with the exception of that of gasoline. It is apparent not only that oil companies received higher prices for their medium and heavy refined products in Germany but also that the prices (which included a substantial tax) consumers had to pay for those products were substantially higher in Germany than elsewhere (except for gasoline).

Stock Drawdowns

In countries where domestic sales did not decline in proportion to available oil supplies in the months from October 1973 to March 1974, oil stocks had to be used to augment the flow of supplies received through imports and domestic production. The change in each country's stockpiles from September 30, 1973, to March 31, 1974, is shown in table 11. These changes, however, mask the more substantial differences in monthly stock fluctuations that developed as companies and governments responded to import shortages. Table 12 shows the monthly fluctuations in crude-oil stocks that occurred from October 1973 to March 1974.

Most of the substantial fluctuations in crude stocks listed in table 12 correlate with the substantial monthly fluctuations in crude imports shown in table 6. The following changes are especially noteworthy.

1. In December 1973, Dutch oil imports plummeted from 1.5 million b/d (the figure for November) to 810,000 b/d. Crude stocks were withdrawn at the extraordinary rate of 334,000 b/d in December to augment the level of oil going into Dutch refineries.

2. In February 1974, Japan's oil imports declined from 4.6 million b/d (the figure for December) and 4.4 million b/d (the January figure) to 4.28 million b/d. At the same time, refineries *increased* their level

Table 10

Domestic Prices for Petroleum Products in Europe on April 30, 1974

(in dollars per cubic meter)

Product	Germany	France	Italy	Netherlands
Regular Gasoline				
without tax	133–151	149	171	140
with tax	347–367	331	389	369
Diesel Oil				
without tax	151–161	104	112	135
with tax	355–366	214	213	209
Heating Oil				
without tax	111–114	89	63	107
with tax	127–131	109	72	124
Residual Oil				
without tax	64–66	54	48	63
with tax	78–80	64	55	66

Source: Commission of the European Communities, *Report by the Commission on the Behaviour of the Oil Companies in the Community during the Period from October 1973 to March 1974* (Brussels: European Economic Community, December 10, 1976), p. 35.

Table 11

Change in Crude and Finished-Product Stockpiles from September 30, 1973, to March 31, 1974

(in millions of barrels)

Stockpile	U.S.A.	Japan	Germany	France	Italy	Netherlands
Crude Oil	+4	−17	+5	−10	negl.	negl.
Finished Product	−71	−24	−5	n.a.	−15	−2

Source: See appendix, figures A-1 through A-4.

of operations, requiring a 425,000 b/d drawdown of stocks in February. A similar process took place in November 1973, when stocks were drawn down by 347,000 b/d.

3. In the United States, the decline in imports in December 1973 and January 1974 caused crude-stock reductions of 220,000 b/d and 290,000 b/d respectively.

4. In France, a drop in imports in December 1973 caused a crude-stock drawdown of 242,000 b/d.

All these incidents of unusually high crude-stock drawdowns, however, were followed by substantial stock increases in the following month, although the crisis was not yet over. In other words, in no country was there a gradual, sustained drawdown of crude stocks. This fact is most apparent when the crude stocks in March 31, 1974, the last month of the crisis, are compared with those of March 31, 1973, as shown in table 13.

In every country except France, crude-oil stocks were higher in March 1974 than in March 1973. Thus it is clear that although crude stocks

Table 12

Changes in Month-End Stocks of Crude Oil, October 1973–March 1974

(in thousands of barrels per day)

Country	Oct.	Nov.	Dec.	Jan.	Feb.	Mar.	Total Change in Stock Levels (mm bbl)
U.S.A.	+160	+100	−220	−290	+250	+160	+4.1
Japan	+61	−347	−71	+26	−425	+154	−17.0
Germany	+18	−27	−43	+11	+51	+164	+5.3
France	−130	+92	−242	−4	+121	−141	−9.9
Italy	+63	−58	+31	−10	−10	−10	negl.
Netherlands	+69	+200	−334	+100	−87	+50	0

Source: See appendix, figure A-1.
Note: A positive number indicates an increase in crude-oil stocks.

Table 13

Stock Levels of Crude Oil, March 31, 1973, and March 31, 1974

(in millions of barrels)

Date	U.S.A.	Japan	Germany	France	Italy	Netherlands
March 31, 1973	244	105	36	55	44	24
March 31, 1974	245	124	47	49	56	28

Source: See appendix, figure A-1.

were used in particular months to smooth over import disruptions, the supply disruption did not cause governments or companies to run down crude stocks regularly.

A different picture emerges from the statistics for product stocks. The data in table 11 show much larger overall decreases in product stocks, particularly in the United States and Japan. This drop, however, is due almost entirely to normal seasonal drawdowns of heating-oil stocks. In table 14, the decline in product stocks during the crisis is compared with the normal seasonal decline of distillate stocks in the years 1973 through 1976. Table 14 indicates that only Italy had a larger-than-normal drawdown of product stocks during the crisis. The conclusion, that the importing countries generally did not use product stocks to augment supplies lost by the import disruption, is reinforced by table 15, which compares product-stock levels in March 1974 with those of March 1973. With only minor exceptions, product stocks were substantially higher in March 1974 than in March 1973. [12]

Table 14
Decrease in Product Stocks during the Crisis as
Compared with Normal Seasonal Decrease
(in millions of barrels)

Years	U.S.A.	Japan	Germany	France	Italy	Netherlands
1973–74	−71	−24	−5	n.a.	−15	−2
Average, 1973–76	−90	−25	−19	−36	−9	−8

Source: See appendix, figures A-2 through A-4.

Table 15
Product Stock Levels on March 31, 1973, and March 31, 1974
(in millions of barrels)

Date	U.S.A.	Japan	Germany	France	Italy	Netherlands
			Gasoline			
March 31, 1973	208	12.3	19.1	N.A.	9.1	6.2
March 31, 1974	220	14.7	17.6	30.0	13.9	5.9
			Distillate			
March 31, 1973	111	12.1	43.9	N.A.	15.7	9.4
March 31, 1974	128	21.9	63.6	69.5	29.3	15.3
			Residual Oil			
March 31, 1973	45	35.3	17.8	N.A.	29.9	12.1
March 31, 1974	47	40.2	18.0	32.3	29.2	13.7

Source: See appendix, figures A-2 through A-4.

Politics and Perceptions

The *Strategic Survey* for 1973 noted that "energy interests and dependence provided the most concrete area of divergence in outlook and policy among [the United States and its] allies."[13] However, a retrospective examination of oil statistics suggests that the supply "crisis" was not really that serious. The January 11, 1974, issue of the authoritative *Platt's Oilgram Price Service* even noted that there was a "general sulk" among oil traders because "storage tanks are in fact full to the brim in Northwest Europe, the East Coast of the United States, and in Italy."[14] But those who would conclude that the supply problem was grossly mismanaged by the community of importers must recall that in the early months of the crisis, uncertainty about its duration and the future level of oil supplies was the dominant theme. In December 1973, a number of countries experienced sharp supply losses that boded ill for the coming months.

The responses of importing countries cannot be judged to have been wrong in the context of the uncertainty, but they certainly were not coordinated. In fact, the only common element in the countries' responses to the crisis was that stockpiles were protected—if they were drawn down in one month, they were usually built up the next month. Most governments apparently found it prudent to try other ways of coping with the crisis in preference to depleting stocks. Their responses to the 1973-74 crisis can be divided into four categories:

1. The "beggar thy neighbor" response, in which governments attempted to increase oil imports unilaterally, appeared in two contexts. France and Italy, among others, pursued government-to-government oil purchases with oil producers and ordered state oil companies to procure oil for the home market.[15] Germany, on the other hand, used its liberal pricing policy to attract oil into its market. According to the EEC, "German imports rose during the first two months of the crisis. The rise was due both to the desire of the oil companies to shield themselves against the effects of the embargo on crude oil exports to Rotterdam ... and to the attractiveness of the German market, where the level of prices allowed the largest profit margin. By January 1974, the German market was saturated."[16]

2. Consumption restraint by means of product price increases or direct governmental allocation of a restricted volume of supplies was exercised most noticeably in Germany, the Netherlands, and the United States.[17]

3. Product export restrictions were most noticeable in the Netherlands, where product exports declined by 15.9 percent in the period of the embargo compared with the same period the year before, while domestic sales declined by only 8.8 percent. This does not indicate, however,

a policy of penalizing Holland's regular export customers; rather, it shows a disproportionate decrease in the amounts of products going on the Rotterdam "spot market," and no disproportionate decrease in the exports to Germany and the other EEC countries. [18]

4. Crude-oil stock drawdowns as a policy tool over the entire period were evident only in France. In the other countries, stocks were used only to fill in periodic severe gaps in imports and were quickly rebuilt in the following month.

Conclusions

What were the consequences of the importers' lack of coordination in their crisis responses? Politically the crisis at least embarrassed the United States, Japan, and Europe. The crisis eased in January 1974, when the Arab countries began to remove their export restrictions. In March, the restrictions were lifted by Saudi Arabia, whose production quickly accelerated to meet demand. The brightening supply prospects in early 1974 reduced the uncertainties that had promoted competition among consumers, and allowed the Washington Energy Conference to convene in February 1974 and ultimately to succeed in establishing an emergency management program for future supply disruptions.

Economically, the crisis may have spawned the decision of the OPEC countries to increase the price of oil fourfold. The competition for oil in spot markets—that is, oil that was not under long-term contract between buyer and seller—caused prices in these markets to rise to unprecedented levels. For example, a group of Japanese firms "won" the right to buy a quantity of Iranian crude at $16.50 per barrel. [19] This and other even higher spot-cargo prices may have encouraged OPEC in December 1973 to double its oil prices: the benchmark Saudi Arabian crude rose from $5.18 to $11.65 per barrel.

Another economic loss was suffered by countries that imposed restrictions on the consumption of domestic oil. The American government estimated that the U.S. GNP in 1974 fell by $10 billion to $20 billion as a result of the consumption cuts. [20] Thus, a relatively minor supply loss had a major impact on the American economy. At the same time, however, the emergency created an awareness of the kind of measures that were needed to prevent such chaos in the future. Principally, the experience highlighted the need to reduce the uncertainty facing governments and consumers about the level of imports during a crisis, and to create a buffer for each importing country between the world oil market and domestic oil consumption. More specifically, the importers needed (1) an institutional framework and a plan of action with which to respond to oil supply disruptions; (2) a formula to determine how much oil each country would be entitled to receive; (3) a common target in terms of acceptable levels of demand restraint and level of emergency oil reserves, as well as an agreement on the rate and timing of drawdowns on those reserves; and (4) a common determination to avoid price competition.

4

International Oil Crisis Management Plans

•

Discussions concerning emergency oil management programs had been conducted before the 1973 crisis under the aegis of the Organization for Economic Cooperation and Development (OECD).[1] The OECD even had an emergency management program on the books, but the United States, which by 1974 was importing more oil than any other country, was not a party to this agreement. Nevertheless, it was the United States that called for a meeting of the major industrial oil-importing countries in February 1974 to "discuss cooperation in the energy field to meet the challenge posed by the OAPEC[2] oil embargo."[3]

The meeting, called the Washington Energy Conference, produced an Energy Coordinating Group (ECG), whose task was to prepare an emergency management program. Over the next six months, the ECG developed a proposal for the sharing of oil during a crisis which differed—at least in its political concept—from its OECD predecessor. The proposal called for the sharing of oil supplies rather than just imports, and although the sharing scheme did not promise to provide proportionately equivalent supplies to all members, it did imply (at least in concept) that in a very severe crisis, the United States would have to share its domestic oil supplies with the other importers.

In retrospect, it is evident that the United States lost little by making this "concession," since the mathematics of the program are such that only a country that is very nearly self-sufficient in oil supplies (as the

United Kingdom is today) would be required to export domestic oil, and this only in a very severe crisis. At the time, however, American oil prospects, or at least the government's perception of them, seemed to indicate that the United States would regain its former virtual self-sufficiency by 1980 under the carrot and stick of the Nixon Administration's "Project Independence."[4]

The apparent concession was motivated by several political factors. According to one analysis, the International Energy Program (IEP) and the International Energy Agency (IEA), both established by the agreement signed in November 1974,[5] were

regarded in large part as a reflection of Secretary of State Kissinger's desire to reassert U.S. leadership in the industrial world; to prevent debilitating competition among the industrial countries which could result in even higher prices for oil supplies and also in preferential arrangements between particular consumers and producers which might exclude the United States; and to confront OPEC with a counterweight of consuming interests. Henceforth, it would cost the oil producers considerably more financially and politically to use the oil weapon.[6]

How much it will cost will depend upon the practicality, efficiency, and credibility of the new program.

As described by a U.S. State Department spokesman before a congressional committee, the IEP emergency program operates as follows:

[in a selective embargo] when at least one member loses more than 7 percent of its oil consumption, but the group loses less than 7 percent of its total consumption:
—the embargoed country absorbs its embargo loss up to 7 percent of its consumption (This is the self-risk element under the program.)
—and the other members share the remaining shortfall among themselves on the basis of their *consumption.* [Emphasis added; see page 39.]
[In a general crisis] when the group as a whole loses more than 7 percent but less than 12 percent of its normal consumption:
—each country restrains demand by 7 percent;
—the remaining shortfall is shared among all members on the basis of [net] *imports;* [Emphasis added; see page 39.]
—countries draw down their emergency supplies as necessary to maintain their consumption at 93 percent of normal.
[At the "second level" of a general crisis] when the group as a whole loses 12 percent of its normal consumption:
—each country restrains demand by 10 percent;
—the remaining shortfall is shared on the basis of [net] *imports;* [Emphasis added; see page 39.]
—countries draw down their emergency supplies as necessary to maintain consumption at 90 percent of normal.[7]

The program can be considered in greater detail by examining individually its activation and allocation formulas.

Activation of the Emergency Program

Unlike the earlier OECD program, the IEP goes into effect "automatically" when the trigger level is reached unless a designated number of members decide against implementation. "Automaticity" must be put in quotation marks because the procedure of making a "finding," discussing it in the various committees and boards of the IEA, and implementing the first phase of the allocation program could take as long as 23 days.[8] This delay is unlikely to have serious consequences, however, because of the built-in 30-day time lag in the shipment of most oil supplies to IEA members. In addition, the first phase of the IEP allocation program is "voluntary" (see pages 46-47), and any imbalances caused by initial administrative dithering can be made up in subsequent months.[9]

More important than the possibility of this delay is the provision that the program will be activated *unless* the members vote not to activate it. Such a decision requires a "special majority," which is defined as 60 percent of the "combined voting weights" and 42 "general voting weights." This combination is required for decisions on increases in emergency reserve commitments and decisions *not* to activate the emergency measures for the group in a *general* oil crisis. A special majority requiring only 48 general voting weights (i.e., votes from 15 of the 19 members) is required for decisions to deactivate, to maintain, or not to activate emergency measures when a *single* nation faces a supply shortfall.[10]

Each member country is allocated three general voting weights, but the combined voting weights equal the sum of the general voting weights plus "oil consumption voting weights," which vary according to the level of oil use. Table 16 shows the voting weights of the sixteen original IEA members, who are listed in article 62 of the agreement, and of New Zealand, Australia, and Greece, who joined later.

This distribution of votes effectively gives the United States a limited veto power to prevent the first kind of special majority described above from being formed. Even if sixteen of the nations vote against activation of the program in a general supply crisis, for example, the United States plus one of several nations that hold more than eight combined voting weights—Canada, Japan, West Germany, the United Kingdom, or Italy—could block the decision. That this scheme of voting weights seems designed to give the United States the greatest influence in a decision *not* to activate the program is an implication we will discuss in a subsequent chapter.[11]

The IEP Oil Allocation Plan

IEA members also had to create an oil-sharing formula. This need was complicated by existing differences in sources of oil supply. The United States and Canada, and soon thereafter, the United Kingdom, acquired much of their oil from domestic production. The other members suffered a virtually complete dependence on imports. These differences raised the question of *what* was to be allocated during a supply emergency—the IEA's oil imports or its entire supply. Rephrasing the problem, the question was whether each member's oil supply right would be based on its share of IEA imports or on its share of total IEA oil consumption (i.e., total oil imports plus total production).

Table 16
Voting Weights of IEA Members

Country	General Voting Weights	Oil Consumption Voting Weights	Combined Voting Weights
Australia	3	3	6
Austria	3	1	4
Belgium	3	2	5
Canada	3	5	8
Denmark	3	1	4
Germany	3	8	11
Greece	3	0	3
Ireland	3	0	3
Italy	3	6	9
Japan	3	15	18
Luxembourg	3	0	3
Netherlands	3	2	5
New Zealand	3	0	3
Spain	3	2	5
Sweden	3	2	5
Switzerland	3	1	4
Turkey	3	1	4
United Kingdom	3	6	9
United States	3	48	51
Total	57	103	160

Source: Article 62 of the Agreement on an International Energy Program.

The members agreed to a formulation that is a hybrid of the two approaches. The oil is allocated in the following manner. If the IEA supply loss is under 12 percent, the first 7 percent is assumed to be absorbed by a uniform reduction of "base-period final consumption,"[12] and the remainder is assumed to be absorbed by stock drawdowns, shut-in domestic oil production, or fuel switching (although a country is also free to restrain demand further). The level of the assumed stock drawdown or other measures, however, is determined by a member's share of IEA net imports.[13] If the IEA supply loss exceeds 12 percent, demand restraint is assumed to absorb the first 10 percent, and stock drawdowns the rest. In this formulation, a member's so-called "permissible consumption"[14] (90 or 93 percent of base-period final consumption), minus its emergency reserve drawdown obligation, defines the level of supply it is entitled to receive from the IEA pool of available supplies. This formula seems more complex grammatically than it is mathematically. The mathematical expression is shown in figure 2.

It is important to emphasize that the IEP formula assumes a 90 or 93 percent level of base-period final consumption and an emergency drawdown rate equal to the amount resulting from the calculation in line 11 of the formula. In fact, a member country cannot be forced to follow these numbers—for one reason, because this kind of mathematical precision is not achievable. The numbers are necessary only for the IEP allocation process. Therefore, regardless of what governments do about demand restraint and stock drawdown, the amounts they are

Figure 2

IEP Allocation Formula

$$SR_x = cC_x - \frac{I_x}{\Sigma I} [c\Sigma C - \Sigma P - \Sigma I_e],$$

where

(1) SR_x = supply right of country X;

(2) c = .90 or .93, the assumed percentage of base-period consumption;

(3) C = average daily base-period final consumption in country X;

(4) I_x = base-period net imports of country X;

(5) ΣI = base-period net imports of the IEA group;

(6) $I_x/\Sigma I$ = country X's share of group base-period net imports;

(7) ΣC = base-period final consumption of IEA group;

(8) ΣP = base-period domestic production of IEA group;

(9) ΣI_e = total import supply available to the group in month "e" of the supply disruption;

(10) $[c\Sigma C - \Sigma P - \Sigma I_e]$ = IEA group net supply shortfall in month "e"; and

(11) $I_x/\Sigma I [c\Sigma C - \Sigma P - \Sigma I_e]$ = assumed country X emergency reserve drawdown level.

entitled to receive—that is, their supply rights—are predicated on a 7 or 10 percent level of demand restraint and the corresponding level of emergency reserve drawdown required to close the gap between the level of consumption and available supplies.

Finally, it is worth noting that countries with substantial domestic production will in effect have an "import right" as follows:

$$IR_x = SR_x - P_x,$$

where IR_x = the import right of country X; SR_x = the "supply right" of country X; and P_x = the *base-period* production level of country X. Countries with substantial domestic production, like the United States, will "keep" their domestic oil and be allocated an import right. One of the controversial elements of the program is that the production definition in the formula is "normal domestic production," not the production level prevailing in month "*e*" of the crisis. Thus, if a country has substantial shut-in production, or if its production is growing rapidly, as is the case with the United Kingdom, the producing country will benefit: the increment of production between month "*e*" and the period used in the IEP statistics will not be subject to sharing.

The supply right resulting from these calculations is the basis for determining member countries' allocation rights and obligations. When an import disruption occurs that involves North African oil, for example, the countries that had been receiving this oil would have an allocation "right"—that is, they would be entitled to receive some of the oil supplies from other sources that were destined for other IEA members, which would have an allocation "obligation" under these circumstances. The amounts involved would depend on the level of the oil loss and on the calculation of supply rights according to the IEA formula.

An Example of the Operation of the IEP

The various facets of the IEP program can be illustrated by means of the hypothetical disruption scenario depicted in table 17. The calculations are based on a 9 percent supply loss occurring in a five-nation IEA.

The example illustrates how IEA demand restraint takes up the bulk (700 out of 900 units) of the shortage, and the emergency reserve drawdown obligation provides the supplies (200 units) needed to enable the IEA to maintain consumption at 93 percent of the base-period level. If the hypothetical reduction in supplies were 15 percent, the formula would call for demand restraint at 10 percent (1,000 units) and for an emergency reserve drawdown of 5 percent (500 units). If the supply reduction were 20 percent, the demand restraint would remain at 10 percent, but the emergency reserve drawdown would increase to 10 percent. The example thus reveals that the higher the supply loss, the greater the reliance on emergency reserve drawdowns.

The example also illustrates the manner in which oil would be reallocated among various types of members. Country E, which has no net

Table 17
Hypothetical Example of the IEA Emergency Program
(fictitious monthly data)

	Countries					IEA Total
	A	B	C	D	E	
Situation before the crisis						
Domestic production	3,500	0	0	0	500	4,000
Net imports	2,500	2,000	1,000	500	0	6,000
Total supplies	6,000	2,000	1,000	500	500	10,000
Situation in a 9 percent decrease in supplies						
Domestic production	3,500	0	0	0	500	4,000
Net imports	2,125	1,700	850	425	0	5,100
Total supplies	5,625	1,700	850	425	500	9,100
IEA supply rights and allocation obligations						
Consumption during base period	6,000	2,000	1,000	500	500	10,000
Less 7 percent demand restraint	420	140	70	35	35	700
Permissible consumption	5,580	1,860	930	465	465	9,300
Less emergency reserve drawdown obligation	83	67	33	17	0	200
Supply right	5,497	1,793	897	448	465	9,100
If available supplies are:	5,625	1,700	850	425	500	9,100
The allocation right or (obligation) is:	(128)	93	47	23	(35)	0

Source: By Dieter Kempermann, who was in the IEA Secretariat when his article "Das Krisenversorgungssystem der IEA auf dem Prüfstand" was published in *OEL-Zeitschrift für die Mineralölwirtschaft,* January 1977.
Note: To demonstrate the workings of the IEP formula, consider country A:

$$SR_a = cC_a - \frac{I_a}{\Sigma I}[c\Sigma c - \Sigma P - \Sigma I_e],$$

where $c = .93$; $C_a = 6,000$; $I_a = 2,500$; $\Sigma P = 4,000$; $\Sigma C = 10,000$; $\Sigma I = 6,000$; and $\Sigma I_e = 5,100$.

$$SR_a = .93(6,000) - \frac{2,500}{6,000}[.93(10,000) - 4,000 - 5,100]$$

$$SR_a = 5,497$$

oil imports, has the highest supply right relative to normal consumption (93 percent). Because it does not import oil, it has no emergency reserve requirement (90 days of zero net imports!) and no drawdown requirement in the emergency program. The example also shows that country E would have an allocation obligation to the rest of the members equivalent to its 7 percent demand restraint.

To illustrate more specifically how the program would affect individual member countries, assume that country A represents the United States, country C represents Japan, and country E represents the United Kingdom. The United States produces substantial quantities of oil, but also imports large amounts. Japan imports virtually all its oil supplies. The United Kingdom will soon be self-sufficient—its domestic production will approximate its internal demand.[15] The supply rights for each of these countries differ in proportion to their normal total supplies as shown below:

Country	Supply Right (in units)	Normal Total Supplies (in units)	Supply Right/ Normal Total Supplies (%)
A (United States)	5,497	6,000	91.6
C (Japan)	897	1,000	89.7
E (United Kingdom)	465	500	93.0

It is evident that Japan, the country with no domestic oil production, loses the largest percentage—10.3 percent—of its normal total supplies. The United States, represented in the example as producing domestically about 60 percent of its total supplies, loses 8.4 percent. The United Kingdom, self-sufficient in the example, loses only 7 percent of its total supplies.

These differences in percentage reduction in total supplies result from the provision in the allocation program that uses each country's import shares as a determinant. In any group supply reduction of less than 12 percent, the first 7 percent is assumed to be offset by an identical 7 percent reduction of each IEA member's oil consumption; the remaining amount is assumed to be offset by members' emergency reserve drawdowns, whose magnitude is determined by a country's share of IEA net imports. If the group supply loss exceeds 12 percent, the only change in this formulation is that the first 10 percent is assumed to be offset by an identical 10 percent reduction in each country's oil consumption.

In effect, this formulation of a member's supply right makes two cuts in normal supply levels. The first cut (7 or 10 percent) is made on the basis of total supplies consumed, the second on the basis of imports received. Thus, in the case of the self-sufficient United Kingdom, the first cut removes 7 or 10 percent of total supplies consumed; the second cut removes nothing, since net imports are zero.

In the case of the United States, the first cut removes 7 or 10 percent of total supplies consumed; the second cut removes an amount derived from the United States' share of IEA imports. The difference the import-export formulation makes is apparent in the following examples:

	USA (in units)	IEA (in units)	USA/IEA (%)
Imports	2,500	6,000	41.7
Total Supplies	6,000	10,000	60.0

The United States' share of total IEA imports is smaller than its share of total supplies.

In the case of Japan, the first cut removes 7 or 10 percent of total supplies consumed; the second cut again removes an amount derived from Japan's share of IEA imports, but for Japan, imports are equivalent to total supplies (in the example only, for in actuality they differ slightly due to the manner in which both are defined). Hence:

	Japan (in units)	IEA (in units)	Japan/IEA (%)
Imports	1,000	6,000	16.6
Total Supplies	1,000	10,000	10.0

Japan's share of total IEA imports is larger than its share of total supplies.

One final point needs to be stressed before the problems in IEP implementation can be addressed. The IEP allocation formula is not an overall emergency policy. The formula's level of consumption reduction and level of emergency reserve drawdown are only assumptions used to calculate the supply right. A country cannot be forced to reduce consumption or to use emergency reserves in the quantities assumed in the formula; rather, its supply right will be determined as if it had followed the formula.

5

Problems of Crisis Management

•

In a real supply crisis, the IEP allocation process will become in effect a multinational, multicorporate oil delivery schedule. Hundreds of oil cargoes of various sizes, types, and ownership status will have to be organized in such a manner that each country will receive its monthly supply right. The kind of mathematical precision suggested in figure 2 will be impossible to achieve, but to the extent possible, imbalances in one month's account will be corrected in subsequent months.

Under normal market conditions, the delivery of oil from source to market is a highly decentralized and flexible activity. The challenge to the IEP managers is to centralize this system *and* to subject it to a monthly accounting to determine if delivery targets have been met. The brunt of the organizing required to handle this task has fallen upon the IEA Secretariat, whose allocation coordinator is in the middle of a network of information flows as depicted in figure 3.

The vital stuff of this administrative system is information on oil flows. There are two principal channels of communication of oil-flow data. First, all member governments have agreed to require *all* supplying companies to report their current and prospective (for the following two months) oil deliveries to government energy administrators in the participating country's national emergency supply office (NESO). The governments will prepare national oil supply reports for the IEA Secretariat. These reports will give the IEA a comprehensive picture of the group supply situation. However, the fact that this information must be processed by the national governments first causes a delay for the IEA. Hence, to get information more rapidly, the IEA will also receive supply and shipment reports directly from the thirty largest international

Figure 3
The IEA Emergency Management Organization

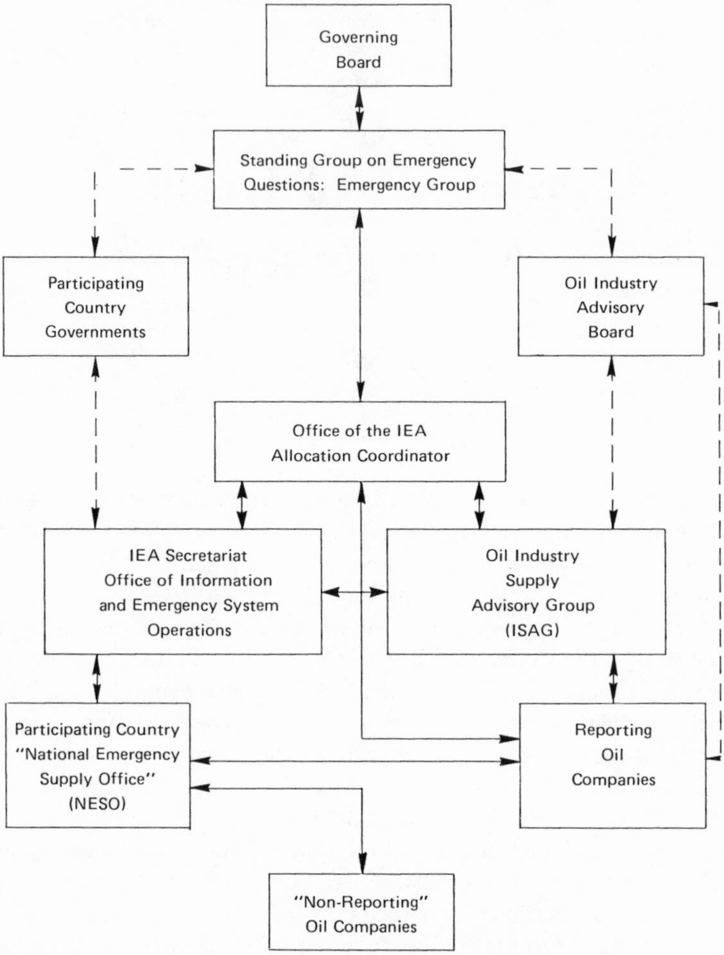

NOTE: Organization Chart courtesy of the International Energy Agency.

oil companies. Prior to the 1979 oil crisis, these "reporting companies" provided about 75 percent of the IEA's oil supplies.

The IEP Test Runs

In order to test the information-flow and data-processing system, and to determine if the allocation formula could be implemented successfully, the IEA, member governments, and reporting companies conducted two "test runs," one in the autumn of 1976 and the other in the spring of 1978. These experiences no doubt served heuristic purposes for the participants, but they also helped identify the faults (in the geological rather than the accusatory sense of the word) in the program as a whole.[1]

The allocation program operates in three iterative phases, each of which can be seen as an allocation program in its own right.

PHASE I

What may be called the commercial reallocation of oil by the reporting companies begins as soon as the IEA governments agree to implement the program (or sooner, since companies may begin to redirect oil shipments as soon as a crisis begins). The reporting companies are to reallocate oil to their various national subsidiaries in a manner consistent with, or likely to contribute to, meeting the IEP national supply rights. Actions in this phase are voluntary. Thus, there is no guarantee that companies will comply. However, the probability of noncompliance may not be as high as it appears to be at first glance, because the less equitably oil is allocated in this phase, the more oil will have to be handled in subsequent phases, during which the companies' oil supplies may be redirected by governments. This phase is not expected to produce a precise allocation among member countries; rather, it is intended to encourage the amount of IEA oil shipments controlled by the reporting companies to flow in roughly the right directions and in roughly the right proportions. It is hoped that the companies will not send unduly large proportions of their oil to their "favorite" markets (i.e., where oil prices are most favorable).[2] The phase I allocation information for the current month, as well as for the following two months, will be transmitted to the IEA and to the appropriate national governments. In addition, the national governments will be receiving information on oil shipments from the "nonreporting" companies, information which will then be passed on to the IEA by the governments.

PHASE II

On the basis of these reports, the IEA Secretariat will issue its initial schedule of national allocation rights and obligations for the current and subsequent two months.[3] A country will have an allocation obligation if the companies' collective intended or actual oil shipments exceed its supply right; and it will have an allocation right if these shipments are less than the supply right. These individual country allocation obligations and rights form the basis of an IEA process called "voluntary offers." The plan is that companies, upon seeing the national supply right imbalances, can make several kinds of "offers" to correct them: (1) intracompany offers, in which further reallocation is made within a firm; (2) intercompany or "closed loop" offers, where one company directly sells to or buys from another; and (3) intercompany or "open loop" offers, whereby a company that cannot find a buyer commissions IEA to find one. IEA can offer this oil to another company, or if no companies are interested (e.g., because the oil is of poor quality or too expensive), it can offer the oil to a national government.[4]

PHASE III

In the test runs, phases I and II did not result in the proper allocation of available supplies to member countries. Thus, these remaining imbalances are the targets of phase III, in which the IEA approaches the member governments that still have an allocation obligation or governments that have legal jurisdiction over "floating" cargoes (i.e., those with no destinations) with a "mandating request." This is a request that a government order a company or companies to ship oil to countries that still have allocation rights, with the hope that the government will accede and the companies will obey.[5]

The three phases of the IEP are not discrete; rather, each month of a crisis can be seen as a cycle with new inputs: new supply circumstances, new imbalances from the previous month, and new arrangements by companies as they adjust to the program. In the latest test run, which condensed two months of transactions into three weeks, there were welcome indications that phases I and II would gradually leave smaller imbalances for phase III to "mop up."

This brief description of the chronological data flows and interacting voluntary and mandatory feedback processes that are supposed to produce the desired allocation amply demonstrates the complexity of the IEP. The program and its test runs raise a host of issues and implications, of which only the principal ones will be mentioned here, since the main concern of this book is how the IEP affects emergency reserve use. The IEP procedure is complex, but the major emergency reserve issue is quite simple: How much of the emergency reserve should be used?

TRANSACTION ISSUES

The test runs were conducted without specifying transaction prices. In a real crisis, all the phases can be expected to be influenced heavily by price levels. In phase I, the pricing policies of national governments will affect the major companies' choice of destinations for their shipments. Countries with unrealistically low price level controls are likely to get less phase I oil than others. In phase II, these national price controls will influence the trends in intercompany transactions as well; companies operating in price-controlled markets may be unwilling to pay world market prices for oil from crude-rich firms. In general, the absence of any price agreement among governments may be the most troublesome wrench in the IEP machinery.

One of the reasons prices could not be included in the second test run was the view of U.S. antitrust authorities that the reporting companies might gain access to information that was not available to nonreporting companies in the test run. The *fear of violating antitrust provisions* most affected phase II transactions. U.S. oil companies could not discuss the prices at which phase II transactions would take place. These restrictions might be waived in a real crisis, but the absence of prices in the test run made the phase II transactions hinge on geographic rather than economic efficiency, causing this phase to work better in simulation than it would in practice.[6]

Product flows between countries were important "bugs" in the second test run. Governments tried to use phases II and III to tailor product imports to complement domestic refinery production. That is, refinery output was not adjusted to produce the proper "crisis mix" of products, and refineries produced too much or too little of given products, creating domestic imbalances that governments and companies tried to correct by exporting or importing products. Large imbalances appeared between Germany and the Netherlands, and the United States experienced (statistically) shortages of residual oil imports. A large part of the problem is due to the fact that nonreporting companies carry out much of the product trade; hence phase I does not have much of an impact on this part of the market's activity.

Shipping problems appeared likely to arise, and were related to product-flow complications. In the residual-oil trade, there appeared to be a shortage of the special carriers required to ship this oil, a condition that in a real crisis would result in large increases in freight charges and further complications in national pricing.

Government intervention in closed-loop (company-to-company) transactions hindered the oil companies' ability to manage the bulk of the transactions needed to produce a good reallocation in phases I and II. This was in part due to the governments' desire to give small or independent refiners a fair share of desirable crudes, but it disrupted progress toward a cardinal IEA objective: to let the oil industry handle as much of the allocation as possible.

STATISTICAL AND ADMINISTRATIVE PROBLEMS

Definition of base-period consumption suppresses the seasonal fluctuations in product demand, which are more pronounced in some countries than in others. This problem caused some countries to receive inadequate supply rights in autumn.

Statistical inaccuracies and delays were experienced in the test runs which could result in inaccurate and unfair oil shipments in a real crisis. "Hard" import data (i.e., from customs officials) take months to assemble in some countries.

Data from nonreporting companies do not go to the IEA directly and may have been responsible for some of the statistical imbalances. The IEA must rely on national governments to improve this situation, but even at the national level, the monitoring task is complex. In the United States, for example, there are hundreds of small importing companies, many of which do not import each month.

NATIONAL SUPPLY MANAGEMENT PROBLEMS

Lack of uniformity in governments' responses to the crisis was evident in most of the key policy areas.

Demand restraint (principally achieved by imposing restrictions on the manufacture and sale of finished products) was concentrated by nearly all governments on gasoline. This would cause overall IEA increases in gasoline stocks, especially in countries like Holland and Italy, which export gasoline; but also in other countries, since refineries' abilities and perhaps incentives *not* to produce gasoline at certain levels are limited.

Many governments had difficulty devising *appropriate refinery yield programs* (i.e., instructing refineries to make products appropriately proportional to the governments' demand restraint programs) and setting realistic refinery operation levels. In the test runs, it appeared that some refineries would have to be shut down, but this carries grave implications for the oil companies affected. If a major company's refinery is shut down, it is difficult to see what incentive it retains for continuing to supply the country in which the refinery is located.

The need for *stock drawdowns* in a single country is intimately related to the level and kind of import mix that country receives in the three IEP phases, as well as to its own demand restraint program and the yield of its refineries. There was a distinct lack of uniformity in simulated stock drawdowns, both among the nations in the IEP and between crude and product stocks in individual countries.

National Crisis Management Problems

Administrators of domestic energy crisis programs must deal with as long a list of problems and uncertainties as managers of international programs. The IEP allocation program will unquestionably help each government's administrators to forecast the level and even the type of imports the country will receive during the disruption. But this important information is only the tip of the domestic management problem. The major part of the problem is composed of other fundamental policy questions.

1. What should be the government's oil product pricing policy? Prices could be allowed to reach their "natural" market-ceiling level, but consumers would suffer. On the other hand, freezing prices does not encourage consumers to reduce the level of their demand for oil.

2. How should the government try to restrain oil demand if the prices of petroleum products are frozen? Appeals for voluntary restraint—encouragement of car-pooling, advertisements reminding citizens to turn off unnecessary lights, and so forth—may have little effect. Moreover, their effect is difficult to predict and therefore difficult to incorporate into a crisis management plan.

3. What proportion of finished products should the government order the oil refineries to produce? If the government program tampers with the normal pattern of demand, it should also tamper with the normal pattern of supply. It would do little good to reduce gasoline consumption if gasoline production does not decrease. The increase in gasoline stocks in the United States during the 1973–74 crisis suggests that this mismatching of demand and supply responses occurred.[7]

4. How should emergency stocks be used? As will be discussed in subsequent chapters, governments and oil companies must choose the overall quantity of stocks to use during a crisis, the overall rate at which to draw them down, and the same for each type of oil in stock.

A thorough evaluation of the best domestic management responses to use in various types of oil supply emergencies is beyond the scope of this book. The purpose of this discussion is to provide an impression of the complexity of the domestic and the international management problem. To emphasize this point, it is helpful to construct and to discuss a crisis scenario in which one country is suddenly confronted by a supply disruption.

Scenario of an Oil Crisis

It is January 1984. Iranian oil workers have gone back on strike to demand that the regime established by the Ayatollah Khomeini in early 1979 be dissolved in favor of a Marxist government. Government troops have been given orders to force the strikers back to work. Fierce fighting is reported in the refining city of Abadan and at other vital points of the oil network. Worst of all, the loading docks at the principal Iranian oil port, Kharg Island, have been destroyed by rocket fire. Several supertankers have been hit and immobilized. Leaders of the striking workers have sworn that not a drop of oil will be loaded until a new government is established. Iraq and the Soviet Union are reported to be supplying arms to the rebels. The government vows to crush the revolt and execute the leaders regardless of the cost. Offers by Kuwait to conciliate are rejected.

The loss of 5 million b/d of Iranian oil could be partially offset by increased production in Saudi Arabia. However, late in 1983 Sheikh Yamani was replaced as Petroleum Minister by Prince Sultan. The new minister announced immediately that Saudi production would remain at 8.5 million b/d indefinitely. He attributed the decision to the government's unhappiness with Aramco, the Exxon-Mobil-Texaco-Chevron consortium that has managed most of Saudi Arabia's oil development for decades. The government accused the companies of mismanagement of several major oil reserves.

In the capitals of the oil-importing countries, and in the Secretariat of the International Energy Agency, oil analysts feverishly try to assess the implications of these developments. In the fourth quarter of 1983, Iran had supplied 4 million b/d of the IEA's total supplies of 37 million b/d, or 10.8 percent. In the spot market, speculators are getting more than $60 per barrel for their oil cargoes. The American Energy Secretary is pressuring U.S. companies to refrain from such purchases. In contrast, Israeli and South African buyers are encouraged by their governments to buy all the oil they can get. In February, Algerian crude sells for $66 per barrel.

In mid-February 1984, the Governing Board of the International Energy Agency meets in emergency sessions to consider a report on the crisis by the Secretariat. The report is offered as a "finding" that the conditions necessary to implement the allocation program exist, and that the program should be activated unless a special majority votes against activation. The U.S. delegates are under orders to refrain from leading the deliberations lest the United States, with its heavy share of voting weights, be held responsible for the decision. The small IEA countries are strongly in favor of activation. Only the United Kingdom is opposed. The U.S., Japanese, and West German delegates appear undecided.

West Germany is receiving plenty of oil because its liberal pricing policy gives importers the largest profit margins in the IEA. The Japanese government is hedging its bets by intensifying its direct negotiations with the Iraqi government for special oil shipments that, although expensive, will prevent Japan from suffering any shortage from the Iranian crisis. Implementation of the IEP allocation program would force Japan to include these new purchases in its total supplies. Hence, its net supply position would be worse with the IEP than without it.

As a result of latent German and Japanese opposition to the IEP, the United States has the deciding vote. In Washington, a fierce debate is on within the executive branch. The State Department favors activation of the IEP; the Energy Department opposes it. In the evening of the first day of the meeting of the IEA Governing Board, the President makes his decision. He instructs the U.S. delegate in Paris to vote the next day in favor of activating the IEP. In a press release issued the same evening, he bases his decision on the principle of U.S. concern for the economic security of all its allies and trading partners. That same evening, he calls the chief executives of the major American oil companies, appealing to them to make the IEP work. He promises that the Justice Department and the Federal Trade Commission will not hinder their efforts with attention to the petty details of antitrust regulations.

The next day, in Paris, the IEA Governing Board unanimously approves implementation of the IEP. In a special communiqué, the board promises that the IEA group of importers will not try to get more than its fair share of available oil supplies from other importing countries. The communiqué also invites OPEC countries to a meeting to discuss ways to dampen the speculative trading that is causing spot prices to skyrocket. The OPEC countries reject the invitation.

In Washington, a special interdepartmental committee headed by the National Security Council is put in charge of evaluating the implications of the Iranian cutoff and the activation of the IEP for the U.S. economy. The President wants to know how much oil the United States will lose, how much of this loss can be offset by "tolerable" reductions in U.S. oil consumption, and how much oil, if any, should be taken from the Strategic Petroleum Reserve (SPR). His one direction to the committee is that he will not tolerate sudden increases in product prices. The American people have suffered enough from the last Iranian oil crisis.

The committee divides its study into two tasks. One group evaluates the international oil market and divides its activities into planning, implementing, and monitoring functions. The other group evaluates the domestic oil market and divides its activities into the same functions. In both groups the planning function takes precedence during the first weeks after the IEP decision. Although both groups have access to countless studies made before the crisis, they find that the various plans available to them do not really fit the circumstances of this crisis.

The international planning group concerns itself first with assessing how much oil the United States is entitled to under the IEP allocation formula. It has no difficulty in calculating that the U.S. supply right is such that the supply loss will be about 9 percent of average consumption during the previous year. The weather during January and February 1984, however, had been particularly bad, causing demand in those months to run a full million barrels per day higher than in the same months of 1983. The supply-right calculation will not take that into account until July 1984.

The international implementation group is up against more detailed kinds of problems. Its informal discussions with logistics experts in the oil industry indicate that the IEP's phase I allocation is not running as smoothly as expected. Some major oil companies are diverting shipments away from the United States in pursuit of better profit margins elsewhere. In addition, American independent oil companies are having trouble securing oil supplies in the world market. The major problem is that supply agreements with some OPEC state-owned companies are being rescinded, apparently because the OPEC companies want to auction the oil so they can get top price for it. Moreover, some refining companies in the Caribbean that normally supply the U.S. East Coast with a large portion of its finished products also are opting to sell the oil in the world oil market. All in all, it appears that the United States will have a large, unsatisfied allocation right at the end of the first month's phase II. It will be necessary to seek help from the IEA allocation manager and from other governments to mandate more oil deliveries to the United States.

IEA reports show that West Germany, Japan, and the Netherlands are scheduled to receive substantially more oil than they are due under the rules governing supply rights. The IEA allocation coordinator requests the NESOs (national emergency supply officers) of these countries to divert some oil shipments to the United States. Japan responds by offering the U.S. NESO a large consignment of Iraqi "heavy" crude oil. The price is $62 per barrel. The U.S. NESO cannot find a U.S. refiner willing to buy the low-quality Iraqi oil at that price. The German NESO offers the United States Kuwaiti crude, which in spite of its low quality is bought up by Exxon U.S.A. The Dutch offer to export gasoline, a fuel the United States does not need, because the government's oil conservation program is aimed at disproportionately reducing gasoline demand. Moreover, the Dutch are offering leaded gasoline; the U.S. motor fleet needs unleaded gas.

The committee overseeing domestic petroleum developments issues preliminary findings indicating that a sudden 7 percent reduction in oil use cannot be achieved through programs that rely on voluntary compliance. The Departments of Commerce and Labor also argue that to force such a decrease to occur by ordering oil refineries to produce 7 percent less will have a strong impact on the economy. The Labor Department estimates an increase of 500,000 in the unemployment ranks. Commerce, Labor, and Treasury advocate using the SPR to make up the entire deficit in supplies.

The committee is unable to reach a unanimous recommendation to give the President. The Energy and State departments recommend that consumers be forced to "bite the bullet" of reduced oil consumption: a 7 percent cut in consumers' supplies should be imposed immediately. The President's White House advisers scoff at the suggestion. They point to Vice-President Mondale's poor showing in the New Hampshire and Oregon primaries and conclude that the President simply cannot afford to jeopardize his party's political standing with an unpopular energy-saving campaign. They recommend that the SPR be used to provide consumers with the full volume of supplies demanded. Their suggestion implies drawing down the SPR by 2 million barrels per day. The Secretary of Energy replies that at that rate the SPR—which holds only 200 million barrels—will be empty within three months.

The President asks for a compromise. He states that he will not impose a sudden 7 percent cut in supplies, nor will he allow the SPR to be depleted by the end of the fall. The committee is asked to draw up a plan that will allow only one-half of the SPR to be used by the end of the year. The rest must be saved for a future emergency.

The committee analysts quickly draw up a plan that would cut supplies by 3 percent in the first month and add a one-half-percent cut each month so that the full 7 percent cut would be implemented by the end of the year. SPR drawdowns would commence at a rate of 800,000 b/d in March, decrease by 100,000 b/d each month, and stop altogether in December. This schedule would result in a total drawdown of about 110 million barrels.

The President accepts the plan. In a televised, prime-time address to the nation, he explains that in the face of this grave national emergency, consumers must accept the need to reduce their demand for oil. Fortunately, he says, the emergency supplies from the SPR will enable the nation to make a gradual transition to a more austere level of oil consumption. He warns that unless the demand for gasoline diminishes in the coming months, it will be necessary to impose a rationing system, and he calls on Congress to give him the authority to impose rationing. This the Congress has repeatedly refused to do because the Department of Energy has failed to come up with a plan that a majority of congressmen consider to be fair. The day after the President's address a Gallup Poll is issued which reveals that 65 percent of those questioned believe the crisis was contrived by the oil companies.

6

Oil-Stockpiling
Policies

●

Oil stockpiles in the six countries surveyed here exist for two principal reasons and are therefore of two types. The first reason for stockpiling is that the oil industry *must* keep accumulations of oil in storage tanks simply because oil is a liquid and there is distance between the point of production and the point of use. These accumulations will be called commercial inventories. They are also referred to as working stocks or operating inventories. The second reason for stockpiling is government regulations: in each country there are laws and rules that require someone to maintain oil stocks. The purpose of these regulations is to ensure that there will be extra oil available in storage to replace losses in the normal flow of oil. These stocks will be called emergency reserves. They are also referred to as strategic stocks (civilian), obligatory stocks, or excess stocks.

Commercial inventories and the physical facilities in which to hold them must exist; the large-scale use of petroleum fuels is impossible without them. Emergency reserves on the other hand, are not operationally essential. This distinction is at the root of the complexities caused by emergency reserve programs. Since emergency reserves are not essential, governments must decide how large they will be, who should pay for them, and where they should be located. As noted in the Introduction, the broad choices are that government can purchase the oil and the storage facilities, or the oil industry can be made to do so. If government does it, emergency reserves are likely to be kept in their own storage tanks, segregated from the normal ebb and flow of commercial inventories. If the petroleum industry is responsible, emergency reserves are likely to be amalgamated with commercial inventories. To complicate matters, there are "half-way" programs in which government holds some but not all emergency reserves.

The distinction between amalgamated and segregated emergency reserves is crucial for a proper understanding of storage programs. The segregated procedure may be compared to keeping one's cash in two accounts; one amount goes into a checking account whose balance goes up and down as deposits and expenditures are made, while the other amount goes into a savings account and is not used until needed. The amalgamated procedure can be likened to keeping the entire amount in the checking account, where the average balance will be higher and the account's ups and downs more moderate. The money is all in one pot, and depending on the fluctuations, the amount that is really "savings" is less easily distinguishable.

The analogy obscures one important characteristic of the commercial inventory, however. There is not one central stockpile, as the reference to a checking account would suggest, but rather there are a number of stockpiles corresponding to the various functions of the oil business: production, importation, refining, and marketing. The functions are connected by the various facilities of the oil logistics system: pipelines, tankers, barges, rail tank cars, and tank trucks. Each function requires accumulations of oil. When oil is extracted from the ground, it is collected in a batch large enough to put in a pipeline or tanker. When the crude oil is delivered to the refinery, the batch is stored to await its turn to be processed; often it must be mixed with another type of crude oil. When it leaves the refinery as a group of refined products, it must again be collected in batches for product pipeline, tanker, barge, or truck delivery. And when that batch reaches a bulk terminal or distribution depot, it is stored to await yet another delivery to the retailer.

Stockpile statistics oversimplify this moving array of stocks by aggregating the individual batches of all the companies into a single figure. When one reads that country X had 100 barrels in stock on a given day, the number really represents something like this:

Crude stocks	*40 barrels*	*Product stocks*	*60 barrels*
at harbors	10 barrels	at refineries	30 barrels
at pipeline tank farms	10 barrels	at distribution depots	30 barrels.
at refineries	20 barrels		

Moreover, all stock statistics provide only a snapshot of the situation, usually the status on the last day of the month. Thus, stockpile statistics are never accurate and are always out of date. The discussion of commercial inventories that follows inherits this deficiency in the data. However, the purpose here is not to provide exact figures on commerical inventories and emergency reserves—that is impossible, as the discussion will show—but to provide estimates that accurately reflect the uncertainties of the stockpile situation, uncertainties that are inherent in amalgamated programs and that must therefore be taken into account in an analysis of the security implications of various types of storage programs.

The national storage programs of the six selected countries differ in various fundamental respects as well as in their technical characteristics. This chapter deals with the fundamental program differences; the technical characteristics will be addressed later. Table 18 summarizes the fundamental differences in the programs in terms of their developmental status (complete or incomplete), the provisions for segregation of emergency reserves from commercial inventories, and the ownership (financing) of emergency reserves.

Table 18 shows that, as of the end of 1978, the French, Italian, and Dutch emergency reserves were "complete," meaning that total national stock levels were sufficiently high to comply with government targets. The American, Japanese, and German programs were "incomplete," meaning that oil was still being added to national stockpiles to achieve government storage objectives at some future date.

On the amalgamation/segregation issue, only the United States maintains its emergency reserve entirely separate from commercial inventories. The emergency reserve is owned by the government. In

Table 18
Summary Description of Emergency Reserve Programs

Country	Status (end of 1978)	Amalgamated with or Segregated from Commercial Inventories	Ownership of Emergency Reserves
United States	Incomplete	Segregated	Government
Japan	Incomplete	Combined	Government/Industry
Germany	Incomplete	Combined	Government/Industry/ "Third Party"
France	Complete	Amalgamated	Industry
Italy	Complete	Amalgamated	Industry
Netherlands	Complete[a]	Combined	Industry/"Third Party"

[a] The Dutch program is complete in the sense that there is no need to build additional stockpiles to meet government storage objectives. The stocks, however, are being "reorganized" to create some segregated emergency reserves.

Japan, Germany, and the Netherlands, there are combined programs—i.e., some but not all emergency reserves are held separately from commercial inventories. In Japan and Germany, the government maintains some segregated emergency reserves (in Japan via the stock ownership of the Japan National Oil Company). In Germany and the Netherlands, "third parties," namely special storage corporations, own and maintain some of the emergency reserves. In France and Italy, there are no segregated emergency reserves. The oil companies own, maintain, and finance the entire national stockpile.

The governments of the countries included in this study have different orientations toward the management of national petroleum markets. On a hypothetical scale, France represents a tradition of close regulation of and participation in the petroleum industry since the 1920s. The French *dirigiste* (state planning) model of regulation is extensive and detailed. It touches nearly every activity of the industry. The Italian government also has regulated the industry closely for decades. The Japanese government embraces the notion of a free market in principle, but in practice the Ministry of International Trade and Industry carefully "guides" the operations of domestic oil companies.

Toward the other end of the spectrum, the Netherlands does not regulate the structure of the industry closely, but tends to restrict its intervention to the issue of price controls. The German government's position is farthest from that of France: it has a free-market orientation and deliberately refrains from closely regulating the petroleum industry.

The United States

The United States presents a special case. It has the most diverse oil industry of the six countries under study here, with far more small companies producing, refining, importing, and marketing petroleum than is the case in any of the other five. The maintenance of this diversified structure has been among the objectives of government controls—at the state level since the 1930s and at the federal level since the 1950s. In the late 1960s and early 1970s, three changes occurred which "fundamentally affected the competitive environment. . . . First was the effective end to [state government] prorationing[1]. . . . Second was the termination of volumetric controls on [oil] imports [by the federal government] in 1973. . . . Lastly was the establishment of an effective OPEC cartel price in late 1973 at levels far in excess of those which had been traditionally charged for domestic crude."[2] This last event put in jeopardy all the firms that had come to rely on "cheap" imported oil. The trend toward deregulation of the oil market had already been reversed in 1971 when President Nixon froze all prices and wages in the United States. Subsequent attempts to "fine tune" the "phase I" freeze by imposing selective controls (in phases II, III, and IV!) gradually led to the establishment of an extremely complex system of oil price regulations that has persisted to this day. This system of regulations has been strongly criticized by, among others, a special presidential task force, which charged that the "cost of Federal Energy Administration regulations outweighs their benefits."[3]

These observations are made here to suggest that although the United States does regulate the oil market extensively, its efforts are aimed not at controlling the market to simplify it, but at maintaining a diverse and competitive market. In effect, the regulations themselves perpetuate a market that is difficult to regulate. Moreover, many regulations are widely seen as aberrations, measures necessary for transitional purposes, rather than as permanent features.[4]

This attitude helps to explain why the U.S. government did not follow the precedent of other governments that require the oil industry to create an emergency petroleum reserve. The creation of a government-run Strategic Petroleum Reserve (SPR) was authorized by the Energy Policy and Conservation Act (EPCA) of 1975. EPCA provides the Federal Energy Administration, now the Department of Energy (DOE), with broad guidelines for developing an emergency reserve, leaving much of the specific program planning to the department. The act grants the DOE discretion to determine the kind of emergency reserve required to protect the national security, although the department's discretion must pass a periodic (yearly) budget review by Congress.[5] Moreover, EPCA requires the DOE to submit a "master" strategic petroleum reserve plan and to submit amendments to that plan to Congress for formal review.

The *Strategic Petroleum Reserve Plan*[6] and the first two amendments[7] to the plan submitted to Congress outlined an ambitious program whereby the U.S. Strategic Petroleum Reserve would be created, financed, and maintained by the federal government. The oil would be stored underground in salt domes or rock mines. Most of the oil would be in the Gulf Coast area, in the hub of the U.S. crude distribution system, where numerous salt-dome sites are available. In addition, petroleum products may be stored on the U.S. (or perhaps Canadian) East Coast.

According to these plans, up to 1 billion barrels of crude oil and perhaps some petroleum products could be in place by 1985. As late as September 1978, the DOE projected that the following fill rate (in millions of barrels) was still feasible:[8]

Year	1978	1979	1980	1981	1982	1983	1984	1985
Amount in Stock	150	251	325	454	623	727	856	1,011

EPCA also gives the DOE authority to establish an Industrial Petroleum Reserve (IPR) as part of the strategic reserve. Under this authority the department may require each oil importer and each oil refiner to "(1) acquire and (2) store and maintain in readily available inventories" up to 3 percent of the last calendar year's imports or refinery throughput. [9] However, in its report to Congress on the SPR plan, the DOE stated that industrial storage of petroleum products would neither contribute to the more efficient development of the Strategic Petroleum Reserve nor result in any significant cost savings to the nation at any stage of implementation of the reserve. [10]

Consequently, the plan stipulates that the federal government will finance, acquire, and maintain the SPR. Some industry spokesmen have argued that the reserve should be financed by a special tax on petroleum imports. Although the DOE is continuing to study this option, it has not yet expressed any intention of adopting an alternative method of financing the reserve. [11] However, it has revised the regulations of the "entitlements" program so that the strategic reserve can benefit from price controls on domestic oil in purchasing imported oil for the reserve to the same extent that those benefits accrue to domestic refiners processing imported crude. This adjustment results in prices for SPR oil that are close to the national average composite price for refiners. [12]

When the SPR plan was issued, the costs of the program were estimated at $7.6 billion–$8.8 billion to design, construct, fill, and maintain the first 500 million barrels of the SPR. [13] The purchase of the crude oil and the cost of transporting it to the storage sites would account for approximately 90 percent of the total cost. The cost of construction of storage facilities and of land acquisition for salt domes and mines would account for about 8 percent of the total cost. The remaining two cost categories, operations and administration and management of the reserve, would require about 2 percent of the total cost. [14]

Since the SPR program was launched in late 1975, however, its managers have encountered numerous difficulties that have caused the program to fall substantially behind schedule. Three sets of problems have been principally responsible. First, the DOE has had difficulty with the selected storage sites. Several salt domes that appeared to be suitable for oil storage have turned out to be unsuitable. [15] This has caused delays in getting SPR oil into the ground, which naturally pushes back the date when SPR oil can be taken out for use in an emergency.

Second, there has been a major escalation in costs. Not only are the costs of preparing the storage sites far higher than expected, but the cost of oil soared in 1979. In fact, the DOE suspended purchases altogether in 1979. The SPR program would not have been so badly affected by the spiraling cost of crude oil on spot markets in 1978 had it not been relying on the spot markets from the inception of the program. The SPR plan announced that oil would be acquired through the Defense Fuel Supply Center (DFSC) of the Department of Defense. The DFSC procedure inherently limits the department to spot purchases rather than long-term supply contracts, which might have provided a more reliable flow of supplies in 1979.

Third, the suspension of oil purchases in 1979 caused the reserve program to fall far behind the schedule originally envisioned. In early 1978 the Carter administration announced an "acceleration" of the fill rate from the original end-of-1980 target of 325 million barrels to 500 million barrels. According to the accelerated schedule, there should have been 250 million barrels in stock by the end of 1978. Procurement and construction problems, however, allowed only 70 million barrels to be in stock by December 31, 1978.

By the end of 1979, the SPR contained only 92 million barrels. In February 1980 the Department of Energy announced it would soon resume SPR purchases. In March 1980, however, the government announced that no SPR purchases would be made until June 1981. The program, according to newspaper reports, was a victim of two political forces: (1) strong pressure from the Saudi Arabian government on the Carter administration to defer SPR purchases; (2) the Carter administration's own desire to balance the federal budget. At post-1979 oil prices, deferring SPR purchases will provide "savings" of over $2 billion during fiscal year 1981.[16]

In short, although the U.S. government claims still to adhere to its original billion-barrel SPR objective, the future of the program must be said to be in jeopardy.

Japan

Most of Japan's emergency reserve, unlike that of the United States, will be maintained in the storage systems of the oil companies. Whereas this would lead to numerous problems in the United States, the traditionally close relationship between government and industry in Japan makes this a less difficult way to establish a Japanese emergency reserve.

The government agency responsible for energy regulations in Japan is the Ministry of International Trade and Industry (MITI). MITI's authority over oil affairs derives from the Basic Petroleum Law of 1962, which gives MITI the right to grant licenses for the construction of new refineries, recommend modifications in refinery production plans, and establish a "standard price" for oil products during crises.[17] MITI does not rely strictly on specific laws for its authority, however, but depends more generally on the traditional understanding that exists between government and industry. It has been said that this relationship is based on an agreement that "excessive competition was not desirable because it would upset the established order, promote duplication of effort, and result in waste."[18] In this context, among MITI's most effective regulatory tools is its "guidance" of the oil companies to help the government achieve its policy objectives.

In terms of oil-stockpiling policy, MITI first "guided" Japanese oil companies toward holding a 60-day supply of oil in reserve in 1972. At that time the average stock level held by the companies for commercial operating requirements was about a 45-day supply.[19] MITI hoped to meet the 60-day target by 1975, but the oil crisis of 1973–74 upset this schedule. Japan's decision to join the International Energy Agency in 1974 established a new storage target: a 90-day supply of net oil imports by 1980.[20] This much higher target would have a far greater impact on the oil industry, persuading MITI to seek formal, legislative approval and authority to require the oil companies to increase their stock levels in a schedule designed to meet the 90-day supply target. The Petroleum Stockpiling Law of 1975 was the result.

This law[21] empowers MITI to "set an objective in terms of the stockpiling of oil for the following four fiscal years." MITI must detail its objectives for each year in ordinances that define the stockpiling obligations of oil refiners, marketers, and importers. In later 1975, a MITI ordinance stated that the national storage target for 1976 would be a 70-day supply. This national obligation was parceled out to the various kinds of companies as follows: refining companies were obliged to store a 55-day supply based on their average product output in the preceding year; marketing companies, a 15-day supply calculated from their sales volume in the previous year; and product-importing companies, a 45-day supply based on their import volume in the previous year.[22] MITI will adjust these company obligations yearly as it gradually increases the national stockpile target to a 90-day supply based on the previous year's oil sales by 1980, and perhaps a 120-day supply by 1985.

The storage target, being expressed in days, will contain a different amount of oil each year, in contrast to the American reserve, whose quantity will be fixed. The volume of oil in the stockpile will depend upon the level of Japan's oil consumption. In 1977, MITI's projections[23] for oil demand and the size of the stockpile through 1980 were:

		Oil Stockpile Target:	
Year Ending March	*Expected Demand: Million b/d*	*Millions bbl*	*Days*
1978	4.4	351.6	80
1979	4.5	383.8	85
1980	4.7	424.7	90

The petroleum Stockpiling Law allows MITI to define the 1980 storage target as a joint government-industry objective. MITI has stated that

in order to promote increased stockpiling of petroleum, private enterprises will be requested to make their own efforts, but at the same time it is necessary to implement policy measures which enable the Government to provide the Industry with various assistance in such ways as financing, cost-sharing and plant siting because petroleum stockpiling is essential for the national security. [24]

The government's most important step in removing part of the storage burden from the private oil companies is its recent decision to commission the state-owned Petroleum Development Corporation (now Japan National Oil Corporation) to establish a government stockpile as an addition to the eventual 90-day stock of the private sector. [25] An amendment to the Petroleum Development Law enabling the corporation to construct and manage the storage facilities was passed by the Diet on June 16, 1978. The corporation's stockpiling target, at least initially, is 10 million kiloliters [26] by the end of fiscal year 1982, 5 million kiloliters of which the corporation plans to store in used tankers. [27]

MITI's other relief measures, according to Japanese oil industry spokesmen, relieve the industry of less than 20 percent of the total cost of the necessary new stockpiling efforts by the private sector. Specifically, the government's measures to relieve the financial burden are as follows: (1) loans for the construction of new storage facilities; (2) loans and interest subsidies for the purchase of crude oil to be stockpiled; (3) a lower fixed assets tax on storage facilities; and (4) acclerated depreciation of storage facilities. It is important to note that this kind of government financial assistance is aimed at alleviating somewhat the burden of expenses, the impact of storage costs on company cash flows. Such assistance does not relieve the companies of having to carry the debt, of having what they would call "excess stocks," which are "dead" assets, on their balance sheets.

The storage debt the industry as a whole must carry is considerable. The storage program incurs two principal capital costs: the cost of the additional oil and the cost of the storage facilities. When it was assumed that the landed price of crude oil would be $13.50 per barrel, the 135 million barrels that were added to 1976 stock levels would have cost about $1.8 billion. The storage facilities, however, were estimated to cost as much as $4 billion, [28] largely because the new storage tanks could require up to 4,000 acres in land-hungry Japan. [29]

The Federal Republic of Germany

Until recently, the German government refrained from closely regulating its domestic oil market. Since World War II, it has shown a strong preference for a market economy operating under a private enterprise system. The government "does not take an active part in administering the operations of the private oil companies." [30] The German market is open to any company that is willing to meet the stiff competition that exists among the German subsidiaries of the major international firms; the major national (and partially state-owned) firm, VEBA; and a large number of independent importing and marketing companies. That competition in the German market is keen is evidenced by the decision of Gulf Oil to pull out of German refining and marketing because of inadequate profit margins. [31]

The lack of regulation of entry into the oil business has gradually led to a market populated by a large number of firms of unequal financial strength and widely differing operations. Three types of firms are commonly described: "independent importers," which are not affiliated with domestic or foreign refineries; "dependent importers," which are affiliated with foreign refineries; and domestic refineries. This structure in itself complicates the moderate degree of regulation that is imposed by the government since nearly any regulation that imposes costs on oil companies is likely to do so inequitably.

The problem of maintaining what the Germans call "competitive neutrality" is particularly acute when it comes to devising a storage policy. In 1965 the government first imposed a storage requirement on refiners and dependent importers. The independents were excluded. In 1975 the requirement was raised to the present level of 90 days for refineries—i.e., the refiner must keep the equivalent of 90 days of his average production of finished products from *imported* crude during the previous year. Dependent importers were required to keep a 70-day supply of their average product imports; independent importers, a 25-day supply (but increasing to a 40-day supply by 1980) of their average imports during the previous year. [32] In addition, the government decided in 1970 to create a Federal Reserve of 8 million tons (about 60 million barrels, equivalent to approximately a 25-day supply of current net imports). This government stockpile was scheduled to be completed by 1980, but the 1979 Iranian crisis has caused a delay.

When in 1975 the government sought to increase the storage obligations of refiners and dependent importers and to impose the obligation on the independents for the first time, it met fierce opposition from each group. The independents appealed to the Federal Constitutional Court to rule the requirements unconstitutional. [33] The major companies in turn argued that the lower storage requirements gave the independents a "cost edge of $2 to $2.40 a ton" [34] and filed objections to the independents' appeals to the Court.

These objections were later superseded by a joint proposal from the majors and the independents to create a "corporation under public law for the purpose of petroleum stockkeeping [sic] which, as the subject of the storage obligation but with the continuation of a free enterprise base stockkeeping, stores and administers an essential portion of the compulsory petroleum product stocks to be kept in the Federal Republic of Germany." [35] All the companies refining and importing oil in Germany would be obliged to become members of this corporation. The corporation would hold the obligatory stocks for the companies, and by being able to take advantage of economies of scale otherwise not available to small firms, the corporation would reduce the costs of stockpiling to the industry as a whole and therefore to consumers. The corporation's debt could be financed by the capital market, and the running costs could be paid by the members—i.e., the oil companies. This would remove the grounds for the fears of the independents that the financial burden of holding stocks would be too high.

After a year of negotiations, the various segments of the oil industry and the government reached an agreement on the structure of this corporation. A bill establishing the Erdölbevorratungsverband (EBV) was introduced to the legislature in January 1978 and passed several months later. The bill was signed by the Chancellor and became law in the autumn of 1978.

The most important feature of the EBV program is that it removes obligatory stocks from the balance sheets of the oil companies. They will no longer have to borrow money or use retained earnings to carry this "dead asset," a point the industry had embraced as its principal objective. In a memo to the government, the two oil industry associations had complained that the "compulsory storage results in an unreasonably high degree of utilization of the financing resources required for actual business purposes. In a number of cases the capital tied up by compulsory storage already exceeds the equity capital of the companies subject to the obligations, in the case of the independent importers even by a multiple." [36]

The financial aspects of the EBV program were the most important in the negotiations. Neither the government nor the oil industry wanted obligatory stocks on their budget. The EBV borrowed 4 billion deutsche marks (DM) ($2 billion) to acquire the maximum amount of obligatory stocks from the oil companies in the autumn of 1978. In this initial transaction, the EBV was empowered to buy or lease as much as a 65-day supply of refiners' stocks, a 70-day supply of dependent importers' stocks, and a 25-day (increasing to a 40-day) supply of independent importers' stocks. [37] Only the refiners would still be obliged to hold some stocks, at least a 25-day supply. The rest of the refiners' obligatory stocks, and all of the product importers' stocks, could be held by the EBV.

To acquire the funds to complete the transaction, the EBV reached an agreement with two German banking consortia. The financing arrangement was as follows: (1) The banks made a ten-year commitment to provide an "evergreen" credit line of 4 billion DM; (2) the EBV can make drawdowns on this amount with three-month to fifteen-year maturities; (3) the EBV will borrow at the German prime rate; and (4) EBV loans will be secured by the oil and the storage facilities, by the annual payments of the EBV's members, and by the normal package of government services to German "corporations under public law," including a government guarantee against bankruptcy, a legal limitation on losses of 5 percent per year, and insurance of the oil inventory against liquidation.

It should be noted that the government responsibilities outlined above are not viewed as specific guarantees of the EBV's debt. Rather, they are general responsibilities the government adopts toward any "corporation under public law." Under these financial arrangements, the EBV initially will be completely debt-financed. Neither the oil industry nor the government will provide EBV capital. The corporation will be allowed to build up equity by retaining earnings from inventory sales (if the total obligation of its members declines from one year to the next) and from upward rounding of members' fees. These fees will be collected by the oil companies via a special "storage tax" on petroleum product sales. [38]

The competitiveness of the German market is cited as the reason why the companies desire the EBV program. The new system will remove the inequitable impact of the storage obligations on company balance sheets, and it is hoped that the impact on their cash flows will be made equitable by the companies' addition of an EBV "fee" to their retail sales. [39]

In the context of the commercial issues described in the Introduction, the most important point about the EBV is that it removes emergency reserves from the financial books of the oil industry. In the context of the strategic issues mentioned, the most important point is that the EBV will cause emergency reserves to be segregated administratively, and to some extent physically, from commercial inventories. Although companies will have EBV oil on their premises, [40] they will not be able to treat EBV oil as their own. [41]

The segregation of EBV oil from commercial inventories should be a clarifying element in the government's emergency management plans. When a disruption occurs, the government will know that the level of national emergency reserves is equal to the amount held by the EBV plus the amount of crude oil in the Federal Reserve.

The Federal Reserve is an important supplement to the oil industry's emergency reserves. The government decided in 1970 to create the reserve for a variety of reasons, among which was the fact that it could not impose the same requirement on the product importers as it had on the refiners. As stated in the 1975 storage law, the government's overall storage objective was "to hold reserves as near as possible to the regulations on the minimum reserves of petroleum products of international organizations [42] to which the Federal German Republic belongs as a member state." [43] The oil industry thus looks to the Federal Reserve to "serve the purpose of closing the gap between stocks held by private enterprise and the stocks required under the international obligations." [44]

The Federal Reserve is stored in underground cavities near Etzel in northern Germany. These caverns have been filled at a relatively slow rate according to the ability of the government to fund oil purchases. The fill rate (in millions of barrels) has been as follows:

Year	1974	1975	1976	1977	1978
Amount in Stock	3	12	26	33	48

France

The French government exercises far greater control over domestic oil affairs than do the West German and American governments. The state's authority is rooted in the "Loi du 30 Mars 1928," which established the principle that "the bulk import of crude oil, its derivatives and its residues is to be carried out under the control of the State." [45] Stockpiling obligations were imposed upon the oil industry in a subsequent series of decrees. Among them the "Décret no. 51-1106 du 19/9/1951 relatif à la constitution de stocks de pétrole brut" required that refineries maintain the equivalent of 10 days of their average crude oil imports at all times. [46] More important was the "Décret no. 58-249 du Mars 1958 relatif à la constitution de stocks réserve par l'industrie pétrolière," modified on January 30, 1975, which required all importers to maintain a stockpile equivalent to 25 percent of their inland sales during the preceding twelve months. [47] This obligation is widely referred to as the "90-day" requirement.

The French storage program has set several important precedents. First, France was the first (among the countries surveyed here) to establish storage regulations for the purpose of having a civilian emergency reserve. More important, the 1958 decree helped to establish the practice of requiring the private sector to hold the emergency reserve. When the Commission of the European Economic Community first imposed its storage regulations on member states in 1968, it did not simply state that emergency reserves should exist; it stipulated that the member states had to implement legislation requiring the oil industry to maintain a given level of oil stocks.[48] Had the French government decided to build the emergency reserve itself in 1958, it surely would have tried to persuade the EEC to require *governments* to build reserves.[49] Finally, France's choice of a 90-day domestic sales storage level also influenced the EEC's 1972 revision of its regulations to the 90-day level.

Unlike the German storage program, the French program does not impose variable obligations on oil refiners and importers. The same obligation falls on any company licensed to import crude oil or finished products. These licenses, referred to as "A10" and "A3" licenses, are issued every ten and 3 years respectively. The crude-oil import licenses, which in effect are licenses to refine and thus determine the market shares of major companies, are currently held by the companies shown in table 19. These major companies provide the bulk of the national stockpile. Unlike Germany, France has a relatively small independent sector, comprising only about 20 percent of sales of distillate fuel oil and 10 percent of sales of gasoline and residual fuel oil.[50]

Table 19
Oil-Refining Shares in France

Oil Company	Percentage of Refining Quota, 1976–85[a]	Oil Company	Percentage of Refining Quota, 1976–85[a]
Shell	15.2	AGIP	1.0
Esso	13.5	Compagnie Française de	
British Petroleum	6.1	Raffinage	31.2
Mobil	5.3	Elf	44.8
Fina	3.2	Antar	9.7

Source: U.S. Congress, Senate, Committee on Interior and Insular Affairs, *A Study of the Relationships between the Government and the Petroleum Industry in Selected Foreign Countries: France*, prepared by the Congressional Research Service (Washington, D.C.: Government Printing Office, 1975).
[a] Percentages given are the maximum which will apply by 1980, and are intended to be generous enough to allow for competition.

The French storage obligations today are less controversial than the storage regulations in Germany for a number of reasons. First, there are not as many product importers. Second, the requirements have been in force since 1958, and all the major companies have had to carry a 90-day level of stocks (i.e., no new refining companies have been established since 1958)[51] and have learned to "live with" the obligation. More importantly, these companies built up their stocks when oil was cheap; in Germany, companies are having to build up stocks at post-1973 prices. Third, the French system of regulations is geared not only to give the government control over the oil industry but also to create an orderly market where companies can earn a "fair" return on their investment.[52]

The French government has not agreed to remove the obligatory stock debt from the oil industry's balance sheets as the German government has done, but it does attempt to equalize the impact of the storage expenses on company cash flows. In Germany, companies will try to do this by voluntarily charging a storage "fee" on product sales. In France, this is unnecessary because the prices of the two principal finished products, gasoline and distillate fuel oil, are controlled by the government. The French energy agency, the Direction des Carburants (DICA) (replaced in October 1978 by the Direction des Hydrocarbures), periodically revises the ceilings of these product prices. In doing so, it assumes that the industry carries a 55-day supply of emergency reserves (the equivalent of the other 35 days being commercial inventories) and calculates the storage costs for inclusion in the product ceiling price.[53]

Only insofar as the demand for French oil increases are there formal plans to increase the size of the national stockpile. There are no government requirements that stocks be located in centralized storage facilities; thus, stocks tend to be widely dispersed and refineries tend to shift their excess product stocks to downstream bulk terminals. In fact, this dispersal is explicitly encouraged by the technical specifications of the regulations.

Italy

The Italian government's intervention into oil affairs dates back to the 1920s, when the government created a number of state holding companies. Among these was the Azienda Generale Italiana Petroli, which in 1927 was given a monopoly to find oil and gas in Italy and acquired rights to Rumanian oil to secure part of Italy's oil needs.[54] Today, after many reorganizations, the state petroleum company, Ente Nazionale Idrocarburi (ENI), is a fully integrated and international energy corporation[55] that has close contact with and influence on the government's energy ministry.

The Italian government's principal oil control measures relate to refinery construction and product price controls. The government has expressed a strong interest in strengthening the position of ENI and private Italian firms engaged in domestic refining and marketing. At present, foreign companies control about 25 percent of domestic refining and 50 percent of gasoline marketing. [56]

The government stresses that it does not envisage complete state control of the oil industry or a build-up at any cost of ENI's market share. [57] However, the government's slowness in allowing companies to increase domestic product prices after the dramatic OPEC crude-oil price increases of 1973 unintentionally caused the "Italianization" of the oil industry to be accelerated: BP and Shell, reportedly because their operations were so unprofitable, pulled out of Italy in 1974 and sold their assets to Italian firms. [58]

The Italian government's storage regulations date back to a 1933 decree that authorized the Minister of Industry and Commerce to establish minimum storage obligations for the oil industry. [59] The present storage obligations are based on a number of subsequent decrees. [60]

Decrees in 1961 and 1976 established Italy's national storage target at stocks equivalent to 90 days of the previous calendar year's domestic sales. The burden of providing these stocks is divided between the owners of storage facilities (nonrefiners) and the refining industry. The owners of storage facilities are required to maintain as a minimum level of fill 20 percent of the capacity of their tanks. [61] This 20 percent fill provision is a unique feature of the Italian program. It applies not only to oil businesses such as wholesalers, but also to any company or individual owning the requisite storage capacity. Thus, trucking firms, electrical utilities, petrochemical companies, and other large-scale oil users are subject to the storage regulations.

To calculate the storage obligation of the refining industry, the government annually reviews the capacity of the storage facilities outside the petroleum industry, calculates how much oil would be held in these tanks if they were at 20 percent of fill, and deducts this amount from the national storage target. According to ENI, the present storage capacity of the non-oil industry storage facilities is roughly 80 million barrels. [62] Thus, a 20 percent fill in these tanks would constitute a stockpile of about 16 million barrels. At Italy's 1977 oil consumption rate (major products only)—about 1.5 million barrels per day—these 16 million barrels are the equivalent of about 11 days of domestic sales. Hence, the refining sector's storage obligation would be about a 79-day supply. [63]

The practice of including part of the non-oil industry stocks in the national storage target, and hence of treating these stocks as a kind of emergency reserve, is the most extreme form of amalgamation of emergency reserves with commercial inventories considered here. It is doubtful that the regulation creates an oil stockpile that would *not* exist in the absence of the regulation. Owners of storage facilities would have more than 20 percent of fill in their tanks most of the time under normal circumstances anyway (unless they had erred in building too much storage capacity, in which case it would be logical for them to sell the excess). For most oil users, the cost of running out of oil will be far greater than the cost of maintaining a prudent rate of fill. Thus, although the "20 percent provision" may cause a slightly higher average stock level to be maintained, the stockpile ostensibly created by the requirement cannot be equated with an emergency reserve in a segregated tank.

The stockpile of the refining industry also does not contain a clear-cut emergency reserve. In general terms, the imposition of an 80- or 90-day storage target on refineries produces a system where, as in France, the excess or "emergency" reserves are amalgamated with commercial inventories. However, the Italian commercial inventory, unlike the French, is affected by Italy's considerable product export volumes. About 15 percent of Italian petroleum products are exported, and some part of the national stockpile is effectively "dedicated" to the export business. The national storage obligations, however, are defined only in terms of domestic sales. [64]

Finally, the increase in Italian storage objectives in 1976 from a 70- to a 90-day supply does not seem to have created as bitter a dispute between industry and government as did a similar increase in Germany. Perhaps this was because, compared with the oil firms in other countries, Italian refineries are getting off somewhat more lightly. It may also be due to the government's more lenient technical requirements (particularly in terms of what stocks may be counted and of product substitutabilities) and to its efforts to enable the companies to recover the costs of carrying higher stock levels. In Italy, as in France, petroleum-product prices are controlled by the state, and ceiling-price calculations include a given return on capital tied up in oil stocks.

The Netherlands

The Dutch government had no storage laws on the books until 1976. In 1961, however, the government did make a "gentleman's agreement" with the oil companies that they would meet Dutch emergency supply requirements.[65] The Dutch oil market and its storage situation are equally unusual: about 50 percent of the output of Dutch refineries is exported and another 15 percent is sold as bunkers for international shipping. This heavy export volume creates stock levels in the Netherlands that dwarf the level of stocks needed for domestic sales. In 1976, for example, Dutch petroleum stockpiles averaged the equivalent of 150 days of Dutch domestic sales in 1975, a far larger stock than exists in any other EEC country. The Dutch Ministry of Economics (MOE) has noted that

however favorable this appears at first glance, in fact it creates a disadvantage. That is, the stocks are not emergency reserves that can be considered available in a crisis scenario. They are commercial inventories that perform functions necessary to the production and commercial operations. ... The Economics Ministry is of the opinion that the Dutch emergency reserve position in respect to their availability in a crisis is weaker that that of other countries.[66]

To remedy this situation, a storage law[67] was instituted in 1976 that required all Dutch refineries to maintain stocks of motor gasoline, aviation gasoline, kerosene, jet fuels, diesel oil, other gas oils, light heating oils, and residual fuel oils equivalent to 90 days of the inland sales of these products during the previous calendar year. Independent product importers are required to hold stocks equivalent to 70 days of sales.

The law also established terms under which stocks held by Dutch firms for other EEC countries can be counted toward Dutch or the other countries' stock obligations. Bilateral arrangements between governments have been pursued to provide an efficient way to avoid double-counting. The arrangements also attempt to regulate the rate at which these stocks can be removed from the Netherlands during a supply crisis. This is important to the Dutch because their refining and logistics operations would be impaired if these "export stocks" were depleted too rapidly by, for example, the orders of a foreign government to bring these stocks "home." Bilateral arrangements have not yet solved this problem fully, and it continues to be an issue in EEC energy discussions.

The Dutch government is concerned about the amount of stocks located in the Netherlands that *could* be utilized in an emergency. The fact that the 1976 storage law did *not* lead to a marked increase in Dutch stock levels indicates that the companies were already holding commercial inventories for combined Dutch and foreign sales well in excess of the 90-day minimum imposed by the law. It became evident that in some manner a Dutch emergency reserve would have to be clearly identified by a procedure supplementing the 1976 storage law. The Dutch government is approaching this problem by establishing with the oil industry a new storage institution, "Centraal Orgaan Aardolieprodukten," the Central Petroleum Storage Organization (CSO). Ultimately, the CSO may hold stocks equivalent to 55 days of domestic sales in special storage, much or perhaps all segregated from commercial inventories. A special tax on petroleum products is planned to cover the operating costs of the organization. [68]

However, immediate establishment of the CSO has raised many difficulties that cannot be resolved quickly, so to get the process under way the government and the oil companies have decided to establish an interim CSO that will hold the equivalent of 15 days of refineries' and 55 days of independent importers' domestic sales. [69] At the same time, the companies will be allowed to lower their stock levels by like amounts. The amount of oil held by the interim CSO—about 4 million barrels—will be segregated from commercial inventories. It is recognized that the remaining company stockpiles will still suffer from the domestic/export commercial inventory and emergency reserve identity problem, but the government is hopeful that the experience gained by the interim CSO will remedy these problems by the time the permanent CSO is established (1981 at the earliest).

Structurally, the Dutch CSO will resemble the German EBV. The CSO will own a large part of the "obligatory" stocks, and it will charge those for whom it holds oil a fee based on the interest and adminstrative costs it incurs. As a first step, the interim CSO will (1) assume the responsibility of stocking the equivalent of 15 days of refiners' and 55 days of indepenent importers' obligations (about 550,000 tons of finished products [about 4 million barrels]); (2) purchase the oil at a price based on then-current quotations from *Platts Oilgram*; (3) rent tankage; and (4) "turn over" (sell) product stocks and purchase new amounts as often as is necessary to maintain quality. [70]

The financial provisions of the interim CSO also will be broadly similar to the German EBV program, with one important difference: the Dutch government will guarantee the interim CSO's debt. In addition: (1) The interim CSO will obtain from commercial banks a credit line of approximately 160 million guilders (about $80 million). (2) Expenses (interest costs and administration) will be covered by the companies for whom the CSO holds oil. (3) The CSO's charges to the oil companies will be in proportion to the amount and type of oil stored. [71]

In regard to the important issue of the oil companies' ability to recover their interim CSO expenses, the Dutch government will not impose an official storage tax at this time. However, it does plan to seek legislative approval for such a levy in the overall legislative package that will be prepared to establish the permanent CSO. Dutch oil companies will be asked to put a storage fee on customer bills voluntarily. Moreover, and unlike the German situation, the Dutch government controls product prices and will include interim CSO storage fees in determining ceiling price levels.

7

Emergency Reserves

•

The previous section indicated that there are three types of emergency reserve programs: (1) emergency reserves completely segregated from commercial inventories, only in the United States; (2) emergency reserves completely amalgamated with commercial inventories, in France and Italy; and (3) emergency reserves of both types, in Germany (although the EBV promises to remove most obligatory stocks from commercial inventories), the Netherlands (where the interim CSO, which will hold the equivalent of only 9 days of domestic sales, foreshadows a larger segregated emergency reserve to be held by the permanent CSO), and Japan (where the state-owned oil company will hold a stock level of about 13 days of domestic sales by 1982).

The prevalence of amalgamated emergency reserves makes it difficult to estimate how large national emergency reserves are. In this chapter, the stockpile statistics of the six countries under study will be examined in order to determine the levels of emergency reserves in countries with amalgamated programs, and several of the principal domestic stockpiling issues will be described in order to provide a partial explanation for the present state of affairs in storage policies.

Commercial inventories are needed because petroleum does not flow from a central reservoir to the consumer. The oil distribution system does not operate like a waterworks, with pipes connecting the reservoirs to every consumer. Rather, oil travels in batches and is purchased in batches. Backtracking from the consumer to the refinery, the size of the batch changing hands increases, and therefore the size of the storage tank needed to hold the batch increases. A motorist may have a 15-gallon gasoline tank, a gasoline station a 20,000-gallon tank, a wholesale supplier a 100,000-barrel tank, and its supplier (perhaps a large distribution depot or a refinery) a 500,000-barrel tank. Neither the motorist nor the gasoline station nor the wholesaler nor the refinery can ever allow its tanks to run dry. Hence, a permanent stockpile must exist, even during an emergency. To determine what part of the total national stockpile is available for emergency use, it is necessary to understand what functions the stockpile serves.

Before assessing the various components of commercial inventories, it is necessary to note that national stockpile statistics in all six countries except West Germany include only the oil held by oil companies at refineries and their principal bulk storage terminals. (The statistics provided for Germany include the crude oil held in a segregated reserve by the government.) The stockpiles in the retail sector, those held by consumers (including the very sizable stocks held by electric utilities, trucking firms, and petrochemical plants), and military stocks are excluded. They are excluded not only because including them would be a great administrative burden but also because these stocks would be difficult to reallocate during a crisis.

The stocks held by refineries and bulk terminals can be broken down into various distinguishable substocks. First, refineries generally receive crude oil through pipelines connected to harbor facilities or oil-producing areas. In the United States, the pipeline system is quite extensive. The oil in these pipelines is as permanent a part of the system as the steel wrapped around it; without oil in the pipeline, oil cannot reach the refineries. Thus, pipeline fill must not be counted as part of an emergency reserve; it is a vital component of commercial inventories.

In the storage tanks that feed pipelines and refineries, a portion of the oil must be placed in a special category—"tank bottoms"—to account for the fact that impurities settle at the bottom of the tank; special measures must be taken to clean this oil before it can be processed in the refinery. The amount of tank bottoms in the total stockpile depends on how often the tank is drained, which will vary from company to company. It will be assumed here that tank bottoms constitute 5 percent of the reported stocks.

Pipeline fill and tank bottoms can be seen as parts of the total stockpile that are integrated within the physical infrastructure of the distribution system. Another part of the stockpiles, which is also needed for the operation of the distribution system, flows "on top of" these unavailable stocks. This is the "cycle stock," a quantity of oil that exists essentially because it is convenient to deliver oil in batches. The optimal size of the batches delivered is a function of the economics and processes of the entire system. The level of demand, the size of the refinery, the cost and capacity of storage tanks, the cost and size of oil tankers or other vessels, and the frequency of delivery influence the size of the batches and hence the average cycle stock needed. In theory, the "idealized cycle stock" is one-half the size of the average cargo of oil received. For example, a 200,000-barrel-per-day refinery that receives cargoes of 2 million barrels would have an idealized cycle stock of 1 million barrels, or five days' worth of supplies. In theory, this batch size and idealized cycle stock would have been chosen by the company because it minimizes its overall costs of operation. A larger batch size—i.e., larger and less frequent deliveries—might impose prohibitive carrying costs on the oil, while a smaller batch size might not be feasible because there are not enough tankers available for smaller and more frequent deliveries.

In practice, several factors cause companies to augment these idealized cycle stocks. The primary complications lie in the irregularities in oil deliveries caused by bad weather, problems at oil production sites, or a shortage of tankers. To protect its business against such disruptions, a company will keep "safety stocks" in a quantity determined by such things as its faith in weather forecasts, its labor relations, and its perception of the likelihood of disruption in deliveries. The level of safety stocks also varies with the scope of operations of the company. A firm with many sources of supply, varied markets, and a large tanker fleet can calculate its safety stocks on a regional basis. In Europe, an international oil company can optimize stocks on a Northern European basis rather than on a German or a Belgian basis. If crude stocks in Belgium run low because of an unanticipated increase in demand, a tanker bound for Germany can be diverted to Belgium, unload some of its cargo there to boost Belgian stocks, and then sail on with its remaining cargo to its original destination.

Some stocks are also needed to prepare for seasonal fluctuations in demand. These fluctuations in demand are more pronounced for individual finished products than for crude oil. Gasoline and residual oils are subject to some seasonal variations in demand, but distillate oils used for heating are subject to pendulum-like seasonal swings. These fluctuations affect commercial oil operations when demand for a product exceeds the normal or economical production of the product during a specific period of the year but falls short of the normal production level during another period of the year. In particular, demand for distillate oil substantially exceeds production in winter and falls short in summer. The most efficient way for refineries to cope with such demand swings is to produce distillates year-round and put the summer "surplus" in storage tanks to be used during the winter "shortage." In sum, such seasonal stockpiling is expressly for commercial purposes, and although it is reflected in national storage totals, it should not be considered a part of emergency reserves.

Finally, a similar phenomenon that also makes national stock totals bulge is the inclusion of "export stocks" in national statistics. This is most significant in the Netherlands, and to a lesser extent in Italy, where sizable export operations require that some stocks be held that will eventually be shipped to foreign countries and hence should not be considered a part of emergency reserves.

To summarize, commercial inventories consist of unavailable stocks, cycle stocks—which include export stocks in countries with large product-export operations—seasonal stocks, and safety stocks. However, the stock regulations of govenments can complicate these already complex commercial inventory operations. Government requirements that companies maintain a given minimum level of stocks are bound to change commercial inventory practices and requirements.[1]

Commercial Inventories and Emergency Reserves

The best way to begin an analysis of the components of commercial inventories is to present the "raw data" on petroleum stockpiles in the selected countries. Table 20 depicts the quantities of crude oil and major finished products (gasoline, distillate oil, residual fuel oil) in stock. The figures are yearly averages of month-end stock levels (with the exception of those for Italy, for which only end-of-quarter data are available after 1973).

Table 20
Average Stocks of Crude Oil and Principal Finished Products
(in millions of barrels)

Country	1973	1974	1975	1976	1977	1978
United States						
Oil company stocks	661.0	710.0	761.0	764.0	861.0	827.0
Strategic Reserve[a]	0	0	0	0	8.0	66.0
Japan[b]						
Oil company stocks	203.5	254.0	266.5	272.4	296.1	310.0
JNOC stocks[a]	0	0	0	0	0	44.4
Germany						
Oil company stocks	128.8	143.3	141.6	138.4	161.6	150.0
Federal Reserve[a]	0	3.0	12.0	26.0	33.0	48.0
France[b]	n.a.	217.3	222.3	197.3	206.7	188.0
Italy[b]	126.4	149.4	136.8	122.1	141.9	129.0
Netherlands[b]	58.9	73.0	72.4	66.3	70.5	59.0

Note: Average stocks are month-end levels (except for the U.S. and German government-owned reserves) for all countries, except Italy, for which only quarter-end data are available for the years 1974 through 1977.
[a] Year-end level of stocks.
[b] No government-owned or military (which are not included in any of the national data) stocks.

Due to the variations in petroleum use in each country, the quantities of oil in stock differ substantially, from 70 million barrels in the Netherlands to 860 million barrels in the Unites States. Table 21 presents the stocks in terms of days of the previous year's net oil imports, a standard measure for comparison.[2] The Netherlands and the United States have the largest stocks in this respect. The Dutch figures are so large because the Netherlands exports large quantities of finished products; thus their stocks serve foreign as well as domestic sales—i.e., their stocks are larger relative to *net* imports (total imports less total exports) than those of a country that does not export oil. Conversely, the United States produces more oil than it imports; its stockpile is thus larger relative to imports than it would be to domestic sales.

Table 21 indicates large discrepancies in the number of days of imports in stock in the various countries. However, the table does not provide a picture of emergency reserve levels, because the working stocks that the oil industry must maintain to conduct its operations are included. Table 22 presents the results of an analysis in which estimated working-stock levels were subtracted from the totals presented in table 21. The assumptions and calculations used to arrive at the estimates in table 22 are spelled out in the appendix.

In table 22, the discrepancies in the number of days in emergency

Table 21

Average Stocks of Crude Oil and Principal Finished Products

(in days of previous year's net imports)

Country	1973	1974	1975	1976	1977	1978
United States						
Oil company stocks	154	123	136	137	122	99
Strategic Reserve	0	0	0	0	1	8
Japan						
Oil company stocks	49	52	55	61	61	62
JNOC stocks	0	0	0	0	0	9
Germany						
Oil company stocks	50	51	55	57	61	58
Federal Reserve	0	1	5	11	12	18
France	n.a.	88	92	99	97	88
Italy	71	77	69	71	77	71
Netherlands	108	129	138	159	134	140

Note: Net imports equal total imports less total exports less international marine bunkers. See appendix, table A-20, for net import data.

The figures are based on the amount of principal petroleum products and crude oil in stock; if all product stocks (e.g., naphtha, liquified petroleum gas, etc.) were included, the number of days of imports in stock shown in the table would increase by 2–10 days, depending on the country. For more information on the statistics of oil stocks, see "Note on Sources of Stockpile Data," page 135.

reserves are narrower than those in table 21, which presents data on the total amounts of oil in stock. The United States has the lowest number of days of emergency supplies; the Netherlands has the highest number.

It is important to emphasize that although the estimates in table 22 provide a more realistic picture of emergency reserve levels than do the "raw data" in table 21, the estimates are only approximations *and* are already out of date. The fact that they are only approximations is repeated to emphasize that there is no firm dividing line between emergency reserves and commercial stocks in the amalgamated programs. The fact that they are out of date is stressed because in three of the six countries surveyed the total national stockpile *and* the emergency reserve levels are increasing as a result of government policy. The planned increases in American, German, and Japanese stock levels are noted in table 23. These plans, if they come to fruition, will change the relative emergency reserve positions of the six countries, as table 24 shows.

It is evident from table 24 that in 1980 the United States will be the least protected country in this survey if one excludes oil company stocks from the emergency reserve tabulation, *even if* the SPR were to hold 250 million barrels, which is unlikely. A 500-million-barrel SPR would provide an emergency reserve roughly in line with that of the other five countries.

It is also evident from table 24 that the American billion-barrel reserve would be the largest by far. The fact that it would come "on top of" a commerical inventory already measuring a billion barrels makes it even more impressive, although the U.S. government is unique among the six in deciding (at least thus far) not to consider commercial inventories as part of the emergency reserve.[3] Whether or not the estimates of emergency reserves are reasonable,[4] the U.S. government will not *treat* commercial inventories as if they do contain emergency reserves, but will rely on the SPR. Therefore, should an oil crisis last long enough, the depletion of the SPR will be viewed as the "bottom of the U.S. tank."

A similar perception of the "bottom of the tank" could emerge in Ger-

Table 22
Estimated Emergency Reserves
(in days of previous year's net imports)

	1973	*1974*	*1975*	*1976*	*1977*	*1978*
United States	32	31	40	38	37	33
Japan	21	29	31	35	38	45
Germany	21	28	31	40	45	46
France	n.a.	62	61	55	59	48
Italy	37	46	42	37	45	41
Netherlands	56	85	93	101	85	81

Source: Appendix.

many and in the Netherlands if the EBV and the CSO are believed to hold the entire national emergency reserve—i.e., if the oil companies sell or lease most of their "excess stocks" to them. In France, Italy, and Japan, on the other hand, the "bottom of the tank" is far less visible; the government may not know when emergency reserves are near depletion until distribution problems occur.

The difficulty of identifying emergency reserve levels is acknowledged by the governments and the oil companies of the countries with amalgamated programs. This problem was the principal topic of discussion at a meeting[5] held at the Royal Institute for International Affairs in London in November 1977.[6] Although the participants did not endorse the particular commercial-inventory-requirement assumptions used here (some thought they were too low, others that they were too high), there was agreement that some such numbers do have to be used to represent realistically the amount of oil that could be painlessly removed from stocks during a crisis.[7]

It was also noted in this meeting that the "identification" problem may

Table 23
Planned Additions to 1978 Emergency Reserve Levels
in Selected Oil-Importing Countries

Country	1978 level (in days of previous year's net imports)	1980 additions		1985 additions	
		(in millions of barrels)	(in days of net imports)	(in millions of barrels)	(in days of net imports)
United States[a]					
Strategic Reserve	8	184	22	250–750	30–90
West Germany[b]					
Federal Reserve	18	25	6	0	0
Japan[c]					
Oil industry emergency reserve	36	41	6	0	0
JNOC stock	9	0	0	189	25

Source: For Japanese and West German net import projections, International Energy Agency, *Energy Policies and Programmes of IEA Countries* (Paris, 1978), p. 28.

[a]The 1980 and 1985 import levels are assumed to be 8.2 million b/d, the maximum allowed under President Carter's 1979 import quota policy.

[b]Assumes no increase in the number of days of emergency reserves held by the oil industry. The 1980 net import level is assumed to be 2.98 million b/d; the 1985 net import level is assumed to be 3.01 million b/d.

[c]Assumes no increase in the number of days of emergency reserves held by the oil industry after 1980. Assumes JNOC stocks will increase from 44 million barrels at the end of 1978 to 189 million barrels at the end of 1985. Net import levels are assumed to be 6.9 million b/d in 1980 and 7.6 million b/d in 1985.

Table 24
Forecasts of 1980 and 1985 Emergency Reserve Levels
(in days of forecast net imports)

Country	1980	1985
United States (SPR only)[a]	30	60-120
Japan	51	76
Germany	52	52
France	55	55
Italy	45	45
Netherlands	50-100	50-100

Note: The reserve level for the Netherlands depends upon the status of export stocks.
[a] As of May 1980, it was virtually certain that the 1980 target SPR size would not be attained.

not be crucial in the management of an oil crisis, for two reasons. The first is that some governments are moving away from the amalgamated type of storage program. Germany and the Netherlands, for example, are establishing procedures that will effectively segregate some emergency reserves from commercial inventories.

The second factor is more strategic in nature, and is mentioned here only as an introduction to the discussion that follows in chapter 8. The argument will be made that whatever the "real" level of emergency reserves, it is unlikely that a government will allow its reserve drawdowns even to approximate the point or zone of depletion. Emergency reserve drawdowns will become more "painful" as the emergency reserve level decreases simply because the costs of running out are so high. It is telling that economic models of inventory systems place an "infinite" cost on running out of stocks. Submodels of the program (those arranging swaps, exchanges, and diversions) provide for the acquisition of replenishing supplies even if this is far more costly than usual. Although the analogy can be pushed too far, this "econometric panic" is not an inaccurate representation of the likely behavior of governments faced with the prospect of depletion of their emergency supplies.

Amalgamated and Segregated Reserves

Broadly considered, a government has four options to choose from when establishing emergency oil reserves. It can (1) create emergency reserves itself; (2) require consumers to hold emergency reserves; (3) establish a "third party" to hold emergency reserves; or (4) require oil companies to hold emergency reserves. The preceding chapters of this book have shown that only the United States and France have restricted themselves to one option. The other governments have mixed programs, as table 25 illustrates.

The variety of storage programs in use raises the question of whether there is a best way, or an optimal mix of programs, that has the highest probability of getting the right oil to the right places at the right time. One could analyze this question in a technical manner, but technical considerations generally have not dominated governments' choices of programs. The technical perspective has been secondary to a political and economic question: Who will pay for emergency reserves?

It is acknowledged by many government oil storage administrators in the countries that chose amalgamated programs that the obligations were originally placed on the private sector because this was the path of least resistance toward achieving the security objective. It was easier for most energy ministries to get authority to require the oil industry to maintain emergency reserves than it was to get authority, or even the consent of finance ministries, to use government revenues for the same purpose. Indeed, in France, Italy, and Japan, the powers of the energy ministries are so broad that it was not necessary to get specific legislative authority to compel the oil industry to maintain a given level of stocks.

This is most emphatically *not* the case in the United States. The Energy Policy and Conservation Act empowers the Secretary of Energy to establish an Industrial Petroleum Reserve (IPR) as part of the SPR.[8] The law allows the Secretary to

require each importer of petroleum products and each refiner (1) to acquire, and (2) store and maintain in readily available inventories, petroleum products in amounts determined by the Administrator [i.e., Secretary], except that the Administrator may not require any such importer or refiner to store petroleum products in an amount greater than 3 percent of the amount imported or refined by such person, as the case may be, during the previous calendar year.[9]

This maximum 3 percent figure is equivalent to 10.95 days of a company's average imports or throughput. If applied to the average daily refinery throughput and *product* imports in 1977 (crude imports being included in refinery throughput), the 10.95 days are equivalent to an IPR of about 200 million barrels.

In spite of the fact that EPCA provides the authority to establish an IPR, and thus provides the federal government with an opportunity to avoid using tax revenues to pay for 200 million barrels of the SPR, the Department of Energy decided against using this power. It based its decision on an analysis which showed that an IPR would neither contribute to the more efficient development of the SPR nor result in significant cost

Table 25
Mix of Options in Emergency Reserve Programs

	Option			
Country	1	2	3	4
United States	x			
Japan	x			x
Germany	x		x	x
France				x
Italy		x		x
Netherlands			x	x

savings to the nation as a whole.[10] The department also noted that due to the large number of firms operating in the U.S. oil market and to the various size and scope of operations of these firms,[11] it would be difficult to design an IPR program that complied with EPCA's requirement that the obligations should not cause "inequitable economic impacts on refiners and importers."[12]

The IPR issue reappears periodically. In recent years, the Office of Management and Budget (OMB), driven by its responsibility to study ways to reduce federal expenditures, has asked the Department of Energy to reexamine the possibility of establishing an IPR as a substitute for federal financing of the last 500 million barrels of the SPR. The OMB was not challenging federal financing of a 500-million-barrel SPR, but was calling for an examination of alternative ways to take the cost of the last 500 million barrels out of the federal budget.[13] Secretary of Energy Schlesinger in 1978 once again rejected the IPR option in favor of the SPR program.

The American IPR debate is another manifestation of the point that in the implementation of a storage program, the question of financing receives the most attention; and it is ironic that just at the time when the U.S. government is thinking of imposing some of the financial burden on the oil industry, the German and Dutch governments are taking steps to remove, at least partially, the burden on the industry.

Placing the emergency reserve burden on the industry is bound to affect the operations of the industry in the long run. Some of the consequences could run counter to the essential objectives of emergency storage policies. For example, an argument can be made—though it would be hard to prove—that in the long run the 90-day minimum storage obligation decreases the incentives of oil companies to maintain a lean and efficient oil distribution system—i.e., a system that minimizes the level of cycle stocks needed to keep all the nodes in the system supplied. A reexamination of the principal components of working stocks will illustrate how a company can optimize its overall investments in the long run by making choices that minimize all operating costs except stockpiling, whose cost is fixed by the regulations:

Stock Element	Steps Minimizing Working-Stock Levels	Steps Minimizing Distribution Costs, Maximizing Working-Stock Levels
Pipeline fill	Dedicated "narrow" line	Shared "broad" line
Tank bottoms	Small storage tanks	Large storage tanks
Cycle stocks	Small, frequent delivery loads	Large, infrequent delivery loads
Seasonal stocks	Versatile refineries, high distillate production in winter	"Static" refinery yield, same distillate production all year

Some evidence that French companies have taken steps to minimize distribution costs in ways that increase working-stock requirements can be cited: (1) All product pipelines of 100 kilometers or more are owned and operated by multimember consortia. (2) The trend in recent years has been toward larger storage depots. More than 100 of these depots are jointly operated by a number of companies. (3) Most crude-oil shipments are delivered in very large crude carriers at the superports at Marseilles and Le Havre. Hence, there are large cycle stocks of crude oil.[14] (4) Seasonal stock build-up is much greater in France than in the other five countries surveyed.

This evidence, which is admittedly insufficient to prove the point, at least lends some support to the logic of the argument that the French style of imposing stock obligations increases working-stock requirements in the long run.

The Size of Emergency Reserves

The preceding section dealt with the size of emergency reserves but not the basis for policy decisions on that size. The equivalent of 90 days of domestic sales is accepted as the national stockpile target in all six countries except the United States. The French precedent, as has already been noted, influenced the European Economic Community (EEC), which in turn influenced IEA members like Japan to adopt the 90-day standard.

Although the EEC is not concerned exclusively or even principally with energy affairs, it has been trying for many years to coordinate its members' energy activities. The task is formidable because the national energy markets differ so widely in the mix of fuels used, the shape of the energy industries, and the extent of government involvement in energy activities. The EEC's first direct move in oil storage regulations came in a directive to the member states in 1968 to implement legislation that requires oil companies to maintain "stocks of petroleum products at a level corresponding . . . to at least 65 days' average daily internal consumption in the preceding calendar year."[15] In 1972, the EEC Council revised this directive by raising the minimum stock level to 90 days, effective January 1, 1975.

The International Energy Agreement was signed in September 1974. Each signatory agreed to establish emergency supply measures sufficient to enable the country to "sustain consumption for at least 60 days with no net oil imports."[16] This commitment could be satisfied with oil stocks, fuel-switching capacity, or stand-by oil production capacity. On the basis of their coal resources, the United States and Germany have some prospects for switching from oil to coal in an emergency; the Netherlands is developing the capacity to switch some users from oil to natural gas as a crisis measure. Only the United Kingdom has the potential ability to satisfy its IEP commitment with shut-in oil production, although there is no indication it is planning to develop substantial emergency shut-in production. The other IEP members must satisfy the emergency reserve commitment essentially with oil stocks.

As shown in the previous chapter, most IEA members had already established oil storage programs that levied an obligation on domestic oil companies to retain the equivalent of a given number of days of domestic oil sales in their storage tanks, but the obligatory levels varied. The minimum level in the EEC countries was set by common agreement at 90 days; Switzerland and Sweden had quite different targets; Japan was on the way to a 60-day minimum; Germany was developing a Federal Reserve independent of oil company stocks; and the United States had no storage requirements at all. In the face of these differences, the negotiators defined emergency reserves as the oil stocks in "the standard definition used by all Participating Countries, which is an OECD definition. They took out an arbitrary portion of supply, 10 percent, as being unavailable."[17] According to the IEP agreement, "that portion of oil stocks which can be credited toward each Participating Country's emergency reserve commitment is its total oil stocks under the [revised OECD] definition."[18] The stocks included are:

crude oil, major products and unfinished oils held in refinery tanks; in bulk terminals; in pipeline tankage; in barges; in intercoastal tankers; in oil tankers in port; in inland ship bunkers; in storage tank bottoms; in working stocks; by large consumers required by law or otherwise controlled by Governments.[19]

The stocks excluded are:

(a) crude oil not yet produced [and] (b) crude oil, major products and unfinished oils held in pipelines; in rail tank cars; in truck tank cars; in seagoing ships' bunkers;[20] in service stations and retail stores; by other consumers; in tankers at sea; in military stocks.[21]

Finally, it was recognized that the amount of "unavailable" stocks may not have been fully covered in the definition. It was agreed that "until a decision has been taken on this matter, each Participating Country shall subtract 10 percent from its total stocks in measuring its emergency reserves."[22] However, the participating countries have not yet agreed on any major revisions in the definition of emergency reserves, and most still count a substantial amount of commercial inventories as emergency reserves.

Testifying on the IEA before a congressional committee, a U.S. State Department official noted that "the [IEA] concept of reserves is one that none of the participating countries is fully satisfied with."[23] The administrator of the Federal Energy Administration explained at the same hearings that

under the definition of the Agreement, we [the United States] have 766 million barrels of oil in hand. If we divide that by our current imports, which are 6.2 million barrels per day, we have 124 days of imports on hand. . . . That does not mean that we could go for 124 days without importing any oil into this country, because the definition of stocks in the Agreement includes some stocks which really are not available because they are required to operate the system itself.[24]

It appears that the countries that had already amalgamated their emergency reserves with commercial inventories would not agree to establish separate strategic stockpiles. According to the U.S. Federal Energy Administration,

when the IEA was founded, those countries [already reporting stocks to the OECD and EEC] insisted on many of the same counting conventions to which they were accustomed. It is commonly accepted among the member countries that the days of reserves calculated using this aggregate stock data overstates the actual days a country could continue normal operations based on those reserves. . . . Although the IEA specified that member nations will have 70 days of reserves [90 by 1980] current "real" estimates of actual usuable reserves are only 20 days.[25]

Unlike the size of the European stockpiles, the ultimate size of the SPR has not been tied to the storage targets of the EEC and the IEA. Early recommendations by the National Petroleum Council were for a 500-million-barrel reserve.[26] In 1974, the Federal Energy Administration issued its first major report on emergency reserve policy. The international assessment of this *Project Independence Report* recommended a reserve between 500 million and 1 billion barrels.[27]

When Congress authorized the construction of the SPR in 1975, its only guidance regarding the size was that the reserve could contain up to 1 billion barrels, that within three years it should contain at least 150 million barrels, and that within seven years it should contain 500 million barrels.[28] The Energy Policy and Conservation Act also required the Department of Energy to submit to Congress periodic analyses of the impact of strategic reserve buildups on U.S. vulnerability to oil supply disruptions.

The first of these evaluations was submitted in the department's *Strategic Petroleum Reserve Plan* of December 1976. The analysis concluded that a 500-million-barrel SPR would "make the U.S. largely invulnerable to a loss of about 45 percent of its imports for approximately six months, with only a 3 percent reduction in oil consumption." The report also noted that a "smaller size would not provide adequate flexibility in responding to the most likely interruptions." A larger reserve, however, "would be desirable if it is assumed that oil imports by 1985 will be significantly higher than 7.5 million b/d."[29]

This last caveat has become increasingly important because U.S. oil imports give every indication of rising above 7.5 million b/d in the 1980's. In March 1978 the Department of Energy submitted to Congress an amendment to the *Petroleum Reserve Plan* calling for the expansion of the reserve to 1 billion barrels by 1985. This recommendation was based on "new data [that] reflect higher import projections as a result of recent reexaminations of U.S. projected demands and supply."[30] These projections are shown in table 26. The amendment report notes that the last estimate (line 4 of table 26) assumes that President Carter's proposed National Energy Plan (NEP) "may not be fully effective."[31] The NEP, the basis of the energy proposals President Carter submitted to Congress in early 1977,[32] contained provisions to impose a "crude oil equalization tax" (COET) equal to the difference between domestic crude-oil prices (which still would have been controlled by the government) and the world crude-oil price. The measure would have increased domestic product prices and made the Department of Energy's "low" import projections more likely to be realized. However, Congress did not approve the tax,[33] and the likelihood that the "high" projections would be realized appeared to increase.[34]

Given the "high" U.S. import level that could exist in the 1980s, the Department of Energy analyzed potential interruptions for 1985 in terms of three scenarios:

1. Unnamed "embargoing countries" reduce all oil exports by 25 percent and deny all oil supplies to the United States. Assuming an IEP allocation of the available oil supplies, the U.S. import loss is estimated to be between 3.0 million and 3.9 million b/d, depending on U.S. import levels.

Table 26
U.S. Department of Energy's Projections of U.S. Import Levels
(in millions of barrels per day)

Projections	U.S. Consumption, 1985	U.S. Imports, 1985
"Low," 1976 estimate	20.2	7.3
"Low," 1978 estimate	18.2	7.0
"High," 1976 estimate	22.2	10.4
"High," 1978 estimate	22.8	11.5

Source: *Strategic Petroleum Reserve Plan: Amendment No. 2, Expansion of the Strategic Petroleum Reserve, Energy Action DOE No. 1* (Washington, D.C.: U.S. Department of Energy, Strategic Petroleum Reserve Office, March 1978), p. 9.

2. The same embargoing countries reduce all oil exports by 50 percent and deny all oil supplies to the United States. Assuming an IEP allocation, the U.S. import loss is estimated to be between 6.0 million and 7.7 million b/d.

3. A "loss of major foreign supplies," presumably due to unspecified "civil and military contingencies," causes U.S. import losses between 7.4 million and 10.9 million b/d.

The report goes on to tackle the difficult problem of crisis duration by simply postulating interruptions of three, six, and nine months. "It is estimated," states the report, "that the likelihood of longer duration interruptions is very low."[35] Given these arbitrary durations, the report calculates the percentage of the total oil loss that an SPR of 500 million barrels and one of a billion barrels can replace. The results are summarized in table 27.

One of the most interesting aspects of this analysis is that the Department of Energy treats the duration of the disruption as an independent variable. An alternative approach, which would have a profound impact on the calculations in table 27, and which also seems more logical in a strategic evaluation, would be to relate the duration of the crisis to the size of the SPR itself.[36] This seems more realistic in terms of "scenarios" (such as those above) in which the crisis is the result of the actions of an antagonist. Knowing how large the SPR is, the antagonist's rational strategy would be to tailor the level and duration of a disruption to deplete the emergency reserve and thus have a higher probability of achieving his objective.[37]

The same point naturally applies to the reserve-size decisions of the European countries and Japan. There is no guarantee that the emergency reserve levels resulting from the 90-day targets will provide sufficient pro-

Table 27

Forecast of Percentage Replacement of Interruptions in U.S. Oil
Imports by a 500-Million- and a 1-Billion-Barrel Reserve
(SPR sizes in millions of barrels)[a]

Duration of Interruption (months)	Case 1		Case 2		Case 3	
	500	1,000	500	1,000	500	1,000
	with "low" 1985 import levels					
3	100	100	79	100	59	100
6	100	100	66	100	50	100
9	100	100	44	89	—[b]	—[b]
	with "high" 1985 import levels					
3	100	100	61	100	38	70
6	100	100	51	100	32	64
9	100	100	34	68	—[b]	—[b]

Source: *Strategic Petroleum Reserve Plan: Amendment No. 2, Expansion of
the Strategic Petroleum Reserve, Energy Action DOE No. 1* (Washington,
D.C.: U.S. Department of Energy, Strategic Petroleum Reserve Office, March
1978), p. 13 (table II-4).
[a] All entries indicate the percentage of coverage provided, with 100 percent
representing full or greater coverage. A 10 percent demand restraint is assumed throughout.
[b] Entries not estimated by DOE in view of their extremely low probability.

tection against oil supply losses. However, many European governments
seem to have based their emergency reserve sizes on an optimistic view of
the probability, level, and duration of supply emergencies. It is impossible
to prove whose views reflect more accurately the security outlook. The optimal size of an emergency oil reserve is, in the final analysis, a judgment
in which one's perception of the likelihood of oil disruptions must play the
prominent part. That judgment is a function of one's expectations, or
fears, about the internal stability of the major oil-exporting countries,
about their propensity to use oil supplies as an economic weapon, and
about their chances of becoming involved in wars.

Emergency Reserve Drawdowns

One other set of storage issues should be mentioned—i.e., technical
drawdown issues such as withdrawal capacity, integration into existing
supply streams, and the price charged for emergency supplies. Again,
there is an important difference between amalgamated and segregated

programs. Considering first the question of drawdown capacity, the drawdown rate of the U.S. Strategic Petroleum Reserve has been determined by the design and engineering decisions of the Department of Energy. The rate really is a composite of the individual rates of the various oil storage reservoirs, each of which holds a separate type of mix of oils, as shown in figure 4.

The Department of Energy is engineering the first 500 million barrels of the SPR to have a "nominal drawdown capacity of 3.3 million barrels per day" and a maximum rate of 4.0 million barrels per day.[38] The oil will be shipped by pipelines and tankers, and the extent to which pipeline scheduling problems or tanker unavailability crop up will determine how much of, or whether, this capacity is indeed *effective* drawdown capacity.

The third 250-million-barrel increment to the SPR (increasing the total size to 750 million barrels) is expected to add 1.7 million b/d to the drawdown rate, pushing it up to 5.0 million and 5.7 million b/d.[39]

Most of the emergency reserves in the other five countries are not centralized like the SPR.[40] They are dispersed, being kept in the storage tanks of refiners and importers, each of which has its own stock drawdown capacity. In principle, these reserves do not need to be distributed to refineries and importers, because they are already there. In practice, it may be necessary to redistribute supplies from stocks if some companies have access to more oil imports than others. Thus, while the U.S. SPR distribution process resembles a wheel, having a hub (the SPR facilities) and spokes (the pipeline, canal, and tanker connections) connected to a rim (the refineries), the amalgamated system more closely resembles a spider web without a core, with numerous ad hoc connections between individual nodes (refiners and importers). In the amalgamated system, there is no centrally determined emergency reserve drawdown capacity; rather, that capacity is the same as the normal flow capacity from the various storage tanks. If emergency reserves have to be redistributed (i.e., if oil has to flow in a pattern that differs from the norm), the national *effective* drawdown rate will be determined by the capacities of the oil transport system (i.e., by the availability of oil conveyors and their ability to respond to abnormal delivery schedules).

One result of the differences between the U.S. SPR and amalgamated reserve systems is that the SPR could not replace the entire flow of U.S. oil imports (which should be no more than 8.2 million b/d under the Carter quota program), while in principle the amalgamated systems could replace the entire supply stream. This apparent disadvantage of the SPR would be telling only if U.S. import losses exceeded the maximum SPR drawdown rate of 6 million b/d, a prospect the U.S. Department of Energy has labeled "extremely unlikely."[41]

Figure 4
Strategic Petroleum Reserve Drawdown Limitations

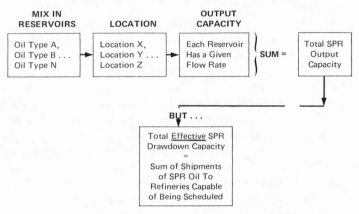

In effect, a big, government-owned reserve like the SPR could be considered a new oil-producing province entering a disrupted international oil market. The oil companies would react to this new supplier in the same way they would react to a new OPEC source. That is, they would evaluate the benefits of buying oil from that source in economic terms. If the U.S. government offered SPR oil at prices lower than the prevailing OPEC prices, every company would be interested in purchasing. If the SPR oil were offered at a price higher than the prevailing OPEC price, only companies suffering crude-oil shortages would be interested.

In essence, different stock drawdown control systems are inherent in the segregated and amalgamated programs. In the segregated programs, the government must make the oil available to industry; in the amalgamated programs, industry already has the oil. This difference is sure to affect one other important drawdown policy issue: the price charged for emergency supplies.

In the segregated programs, the government has the opportunity to set a separate price for emergency supplies. The U.S. government, for example, could price the oil at the same level as domestic crude oil (which through government controls has been kept well under OPEC price levels), at the same level as OPEC oil prices, or at the spot-market prices, which in a disruption can be substantially higher than OPEC levels.

The reaction of the oil industry to the sale of SPR oil is important because it can indirectly affect U.S. import levels. If SPR oil were priced lower than OPEC oil, companies would have an economic incentive to use the SPR to meet their U.S. oil requirements, thus freeing some of the OPEC supplies for foreign markets. If SPR oil were priced higher than

OPEC oil, the companies' incentive would be the opposite, and those companies with access to OPEC oil would prefer to meet their U.S. supply requirements with OPEC oil.

The price set for U.S. SPR oil could also influence OPEC prices. If OPEC countries saw that the U.S. government was earning a premium by selling its oil at a price above the OPEC level, they would likely be encouraged to raise their prices to the "SPR price." Even though this would be only a pretext for an action they would have taken anyway, importing countries' pleas for OPEC price restraint during a crisis would seem hypocritical if the U.S. government showed no such price restraint.

Hence, it appears that the best policy during a disruption would be to sell SPR oil at prevailing OPEC prices. This observation applies equally to the oil sold from government stocks in Japan and Germany. In fact, this policy appears to be rational for the IEA as a group. If the IEA governments refrained from collecting the maximum tax revenues from the sale of emergency supplies, two benefits could ensue. First, they might thereby encourage OPEC countries to moderate their price increases, and they might dampen speculation in the spot markets as well. Second, a uniform emergency supply price could also make it easier for oil companies to distribute imports fairly: if there were no emergency supply bargains to be had, there would be fewer incentives to over- or undersupply particular importing countries.

8

The Oil Security
Outlook

•

In the 1980s the oil security of the importing countries will be determined by the state of the world oil market and by the countries' preparedness for sudden oil disruptions. Two key elements of preparedness are the IEA allocation program and the members' national emergency petroleum reserves. The purpose of these programs is to enable governments to manage the impact that a sudden oil supply disruption has on society. The kind of influence governments will try to exert depends on their objectives, which in turn will be shaped by officials' perceptions of the circumstances. In some circumstances, governments may believe that they can prevent any damage to their societies; in others, they may believe some damage is unavoidable and will try to influence where, when, and how damage occurs.

An Examination of Vulnerability

The vulnerability problem is complex because the economy is complex. The economic history of the 1970s vividly illustrates the difficulty governments have had in managing economic growth, inflation, and employment. Along with labor and capital, energy is a key input, but it is practically impossible to predict what would happen if a given amount of energy were removed. The difficulty stems from the variety of uses to which energy is put, and from the economy's ability to substitute, to some extent, one form of energy for another, as well as labor and capital for energy. The variety of energy uses complicates vulnerability analysis because some energy uses contribute more to quantifiable economic activities (e.g., production, employment) than other uses do. For example, the chemical industry uses energy to keep offices warm or cool, to heat furnaces and coolers in the manufacturing process, as raw materials, and as fuel for the vehicles that deliver its goods. If the chemical industry were suddenly confronted with a 10 percent energy loss, it might be able to offset this loss simply by keeping offices warmer or colder, and there would be little, if any, impact on the industry's production. If such measures did not offset the loss, production would most likely suffer.

Energy sources can sometimes be substituted for one another. An electric power plant, for example, may be able to use natural gas in place of oil. Moreover, there may be sectors of the economy in which capital or labor can be substituted for energy. A homeowner can improve the insulation of his house to cut down on heating or cooling requirements. A dairy farm can use laborers in place of milking machines (an alternative that may be more feasible than it seems if the farmer's neighbors are unable to get to work due to a gasoline shortage).

Germany and France provide an illustration of the effects of a severe curtailment of oil supplies on various economic sectors.[1] Table 28 shows surprisingly small differences in the percentage of total oil supplies demanded by the various sectors in the two countries, indicating that an equivalent loss of oil might have a relatively similar effect on the two economies. However, when one looks at each sector's utilization of oil in relation to other energy sources (table 29), several striking differences become apparent. In the case of the two important productive sectors, industry and electric power, France relies more heavily on oil—and imported oil at that—than Germany does. This is particularly evident in the electric power industry. The difference results from the decision by the German government over the past two decades to maintain domestic coal production, whereas French governments have allowed coal production to give way to cheaper imported oil. Equivalent disruptions of oil imports would therefore be more damaging to the French economy than to the German.

A picture of the impact of oil losses can be obtained by considering how a hypothetical disruption could be allocated among the sectors. If both countries lost 40 percent of their oil supplies for an undetermined period, one possible allocation of the shortage would be that shown in table 30. Although this is but one of many potential allocation schemes, it does illustrate the nature of the problem governments face. The agricultural sector uses little oil, but its supplies are clearly vital. The extent to which oil can be conserved in the industrial and electric sectors is relatively fixed, since governments would be extremely reluctant to allow any oil supply disruption to cause a decline in industrial pro-

Table 28

French and West German Sectoral Oil Consumption
as percentage of Total Oil Consumption, 1973

Sector	France	Germany
Agriculture	2.9	1.1
Heavy Industry	14.7	22.1
Power Plants	12.4	5.7
Light Industry	23.0	15.7
Heating	23.7	34.2
Transport	23.3	21.1

Source: *Statistics of Energy, 1959-1973* (Paris: Economic
Statistics and National Accounts Division, Organization for
Economic Cooperation and Development, 1974).

Table 29

Percentage of French and West German Sectoral
Energy Demand Met by Oil, 1973

Sector	France	Germany
Agriculture	n.a.	n.a.
All Industry	61.1	49.6
Power Plants	59.2	8.9
Heating	65.8	62.2
Transport	100.0	100.0

Source: Same as for table 28.

duction. The greatest potential for conservation therefore lies in the heating and transport sectors. In the private transport sector, the 55 percent supply loss stipulated in table 30 would require drastic changes in life styles. There are various ways to take advantage of the potential conservation in this sector: for instance, to prevent maldistribution of supplies a "white market" could be created. Gasoline-rationing coupons could be issued in numbers equivalent to the total number of motorists, and those who needed more would be allowed to purchase coupons from others who were willing to sell them. Although the ability of an industrial society to adjust to such changes has not really been tested—not even in 1973—it does seem possible that even a 50 percent cut in fuel could be achieved in this sector without severe economic effects because there are substitutes for the automobile (especially in Europe, where train service is extensive) and because much automobile use can be temporarily curtailed without directly affecting employment and production, except, of course, in the car service industry.[2]

Table 30
Possible Allocation Given a 40 Percent Reduction in
French and West German Oil Supplies

Sector	Percent Reduction in Sector Supplies	Percent Contribution to Reduction in Overall Supplies	
		France	Germany
Agriculture	10	0.3	0.1
Heavy Industry	30	4.4	6.6
Power Plants	35	4.3	2.0
Light Industry	40	9.2	6.3
Heating	45	10.7	15.4
Transport	55	12.8	11.6
Total		41.7	42.0

The same cannot be said for the heating sector. The time of year when the supply reduction occurred and the weather would be complicating factors. Curtailing heating-oil requirements by 45 percent would have more of a differential impact on consumers than would gasoline curtailments, because those who do not use oil for heating would not be affected at all. Furthermore, any government would come under severe pressure to prevent suffering, and although curtailing 45 percent of a consumer's heating oil does not mean that he would necessarily be 45 percent less warm, the unpredictability of the weather and the nature of the consequences of heating-oil shortages would make it difficult to take advantage of the considerable potential for conservation that exists.

The differences in vulnerability between France and Germany are more pronounced in the industrial sector than in transport and heating. A 35 percent oil loss would not affect Germany's overall electricity production severely, since that production is substantially based on coal, but such a reduction would have a very significant effect on the French electric power system and might even require electricity to be rationed, as occurred in Britain in 1973–74.

The adaptability of industry to energy shortages is a key to the overall vulnerability of an economy. Within the manufacturing sector, some industries are more vulnerable than others, and within industries, some firms are more vulnerable than others. A company's vulnerability is largely a matter of whether it uses oil as a direct feedstock, as in the production of chemicals; for process heating, as in glassmaking; or for space heating, as in engineering or assembly plants.

Despite the ability of most industries to make some adjustments, a 30 percent oil loss to the heavy industries (including those which use oil as a feedstock or for process heating) would be almost certain to result in production losses. Many of these industries have already increased their efficiency in response to the 1973 price increases. If the iron and steel, chemical, textile, and cement industries, which provide the basic goods of the industrial societies, had to be deprived of oil supplies because the other sectors of the economy were being stretched to their limits, an oil import reduction would become more than an inconvenience. Industrial output would fall, and orders would have to be met from inventories until, when these were exhausted, the inability of subsidiary or downstream industries to get the basic elements of their operations would cause their output to decline. As a consequence, production and employment losses would rise very quickly.

It is safe to conclude from this discussion that a 40 percent reduction in supplies to France and Germany would cause a considerable loss in production. In theory, one might be able to identify a level and duration of oil supply loss that could be labeled "tolerable" or "less than severe," and argue that anything less should not be considered a security threat. Conversely, there is a "zone" where the economic effects of a reduction begin to pile on top of one another, and where production and employment begin to decrease exponentially and no doubt alarmingly.

An analysis of the vulnerability of the American economy to sudden oil losses was presented by the U.S. Federal Energy Administration (FEA) in the *Strategic Petroleum Reserve Plan* of December 1976. The FEA estimated that a 7 percent loss of oil supplies would cause a 0.9 percent decrease in the GNP, which for a $2 trillion GNP amounts to an $18 billion loss.[3] In effect, the FEA implied that there is no "free" demand restraint. This reasoning was behind the FEA's comment that

It will be difficult to identify acceptable actions that will result in reductions substantially above 3 percent [of normal domestic oil demand] without severe economic impacts. ... The attainment of seven and ten percent demand restraint levels [as called for by the IEA program] could only be achieved over an extended period of time. ... Such reductions are likely to require gasoline rationing and other fairly severe measures.[4]

The FEA report mentions that the IEA agreement allows participating countries to "use emergency petroleum reserves held in excess of their emergency reserve commitment, rather than take the reductions in consumption," and suggests that U.S. consumption during a crisis be reduced "on a linear basis throughout the duration of the interruption to obtain a 3 percent reduction after three months and a 6 percent reduction after six months."[5]

If the FEA's assessment is correct, even the "limited disruptions" requiring only a 7 percent demand restraint could be quite damaging.

Moreover, the United States is considered to use oil less efficiently—i.e., derive less GNP from its oil supplies—than do most other importers. If so, Europe and Japan would suffer greater proportional GNP losses from oil shortages.

To avoid these losses, governments may be tempted to use emergency reserves even in a 7 percent oil disruption. Japan, as discussed previously, is planning a 60-million-barrel extra reserve by 1985, possibly to avoid demand restraint. The Japanese government is concerned about the costs of a 7 or 10 percent demand restraint, not only because the Japanese are among the most efficient oil consumers, but also because Japan continues to have a higher oil demand growth rate than do many other industrial countries. If the oil demand growth rate were 6 percent per annum when a disruption struck, the 7 or 10 percent demand restraint imposed at the beginning of the crisis would effectively increase by 1 percent every two months.

Emergency Reserve Drawdowns

If the demand restraint called for by the IEP were considered too severe by importing governments, their only recourse, short of dropping out of the allocation program in the hopes of getting more oil in the market, would be to increase the rate of emergency reserve drawdowns. The reserves, however, provide a finite source of alternative supplies, and accelerating the drawdown rate in order to avoid demand restraint would increase the danger of depleting the reserves.

Governments' reluctance to run down stocks was apparent in the 1973–74 crisis. That reluctance reappeared recently in the actions of U.S. electric utilities during the coal strike of early 1978. Newspaper reports indicated that the Pennsylvania–New Jersey–Maryland "power pool" had an overall stock of coal equivalent to 80 days of their requirements, but a contingency plan was "to go into effect at a 45-day level . . . for conversions from coal to oil and halving output of coal-fired generators. At a 30-day level, coal burning generators would be reduced to only plant protection level of output."[6]

In oil, as in coal emergency management, it is inconceivable that a steady drain of emergency reserves would not affect government perceptions of and responses to the crisis. The reaction will be strongest when it appears that the disruption may be "open ended." In these situations, early confidence in the adequacy of reserves will give way to concern about the consequences of a large drop in stock levels. This concern is likely to appear first in countries whose emergency reserves are amalgamated with oil company working stocks. Uncertainty about when the decrease in stock levels will cause distribution problems, spot shortages, refinery closings, and other manifestations of inadequate stock levels will increase concern and anxiety. That governments will find it difficult to predict when these things will occur may make them cautious about drawing down stocks well before emergency reserves are depleted.

The IEA agreement addresses this problem in articles 15 and 20, which state that when "cumulative daily emergency reserve drawdown obligations ... have reached 50 percent of emergency reserve commitments, ... the [IEA Management] Committee shall report to the Governing Board ... proposing measures required for meeting the necessities of the situation."[7] However, pressure for such a reconsideration is likely to come well before the 50 percent point specified in the agreement. In many countries, commercial inventories are estimated to be the equivalent of about 45 days of imports, so some countries will not want to wait until stocks are down to the 45-day level to reassess the level of demand restraint.

Emergency reserve drawdown planning is, analytically, closely related to the problem of demand restraint planning. In essence, the availability of emergency reserves gives governments some leeway in planning how to help the economy adjust to sudden losses in normal oil flows. The government has three drawdown options, all of which are circumscribed by the amount of emergency supplies available: (1) use emergency supplies at a constant rate to offset the entire shortage; (2) use emergency reserves at a constant rate to offset part of the shortage; and (3) use emergency reserves at a gradually decreasing rate to offset the shortage.

These three alternatives are depicted in figure 5. The three alternatives are not, of course, mutually exclusive. Alternative 1 can be used for a few months, then alternative 2, then 3.

The decision on which alternative to use is likely to be influenced first of all by the government's perception of the duration of the crisis, the amount of oil that will be lost, and the amount of emergency reserves the government is willing to commit to this particular disruption. To take a simple example, if the U.S. Alaska pipeline had to be shut down for six months, and foreign oil could not be found to replace this flow, a U.S. government decision to use its SPR to offset the loss completely would not be surprising. This would be a disruption with a technically limited, as opposed to a politically open-ended, duration. Another Arab oil embargo would be a totally different case. If it were viewed as potentially open-ended, the government would likely choose alternative 3, employing SPR oil to allow the economy to make a gradual transition to a lower level of oil consumption.

The open-ended disruption poses the most difficult policy questions.

Figure 5
Alternative Emergency Reserve Drawdown Schedules

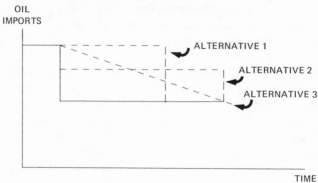

One of the most difficult is how much oil to plan to keep in stock. Formal, quantitative analysis is of little use here, because the central problem in the decision is the likelihood that another supply disruption will occur after the current one is over. The more oil is removed from emergency stocks, the more damaging another disruption would be. The threat of a subsequent disruption would be less troubling if governments could be sure that they could rebuild emergency stocks after the first disruption. Such certainty, however, is not likely to exist.[8]

The desire to keep emergency supplies in storage conflicts with the desire to minimize demand restraint, or even with alternative 3, a drawdown policy that gradually increases demand restraint. It is necessary to point out, however, that the future difference in IEA-country stock levels will give some individual governments greater leeway than others. By 1985 the United States and Japan (and the Netherlands, if one counts "export" stocks) may have considerably more than the IEA's target 90-day storage level. Under the IEP's "rules," these countries may use their "surplus" reserves in place of demand restraint (i.e., they could follow alternatives 1 or 3). Countries like Germany and Italy will not be able to take advantage of this option to the same extent, if at all, because their reserves are so close to the 90-day level.

This difference raises two problems. The first is the simple difference in economic damage or endurance potential. If Germany and Italy restrained demand by 7 or 10 percent, and the others did not, Germany and Italy would be likely to suffer greater economic losses. If they did not restrain demand by 7 or 10 percent, but followed drawdown alternatives 1 or 3, their endurance potential would suffer in comparison to that of the others. That is, Germany and Italy would be in danger of running out of emergency reserves long before the other countries ran out.

The problem, of course, with the emergency reserve drawdown problem is the necessity of stringing together numerous "ifs" to make a point. Disruptions may never occur, Germany may be capable of restraining demand by 20 percent, and so forth. The major conclusion from these observations, therefore, must be a characterization of the limits to the utility of emergency reserve drawdowns. They are not a free commodity; to the contrary, the cost of using each successive barrel increases.

Endurance of Emergency Reserves

An estimate of the utility of emergency reserves can be obtained by performing several simple calculations. Assume that each IEA member country has the equivalent of a given number of days of net imports in emergency reserves, that each country abides by the IEA demand restraint levels, and that no oil distribution problems arise as IEA reserves are drawn down.

As noted previously, the IEP recommends that members make demand restraint the first line of defense, and emergency reserve drawdowns the second line of defense, against oil import losses. If countries abide by these recommendations, a 9 percent IEA oil supply loss, such as occurred in the 1973–74 crisis, would call for an emergency reserve drawdown equivalent to only 2 percent of normal IEA consumption (with demand restraint absorbing the first 7 percent). If the IEA countries had 60 days' worth of net oil imports in emergency reserves, a daily drawdown obligation of 2 percent of consumption (equivalent to 3.3 percent of daily net imports)[9] would deplete the 60-day emergency reserve in about *1,800 days*, or nearly five years (the figure results from dividing 60 by 0.033).

To define the importers' ability to endure larger oil supply losses and thereby create more substantial emergency reserve drawdowns, several calculations are needed. First, the emergency reserve drawdowns and the number of days required to exhaust 30, 45, and 60 days' worth of stocks (equivalent to net imports) can be estimated as above. The results are presented in table 31. These calculations clearly depict the way emergency reserve drawdowns become more important as the size of the supply loss increases, and how sharply the stocks fall (in terms of the number of days the disruption must last to deplete a 30-, 45-, and 60-day supply of stocks) once the supply loss exceeds 10 percent.

What is the likelihood that supply curtailments greater than 10 percent will occur? Although an assessment of the probabilities of oil supply losses is beyond the scope of this study, the kinds of oil supply reductions that would cause the IEA to make large emergency reserve drawdowns can be defined.

IEA and OECD oil data for the period July 1, 1976, to June 30, 1977 (table 32) show that a 10 percent loss of the IEA's available supplies during this period would have averaged 3.6 million b/d; a 15 percent loss, 5.4 million b/d. IEA data on imports for the same period (table 33) indicate the levels of supply provided by specific producers. OPEC provided 74 percent of IEA's gross imports, or 20 million b/d; Arab OPEC countries provided 44 percent, or 12 million b/d; and Saudi Arabia, Kuwait, Libya, and the United Arab Emirates (UAE), who cut their production to begin the 1973–74 oil crisis, provided 36 percent, or 9.8 million b/d. By combining the IEA supply and import data, it is possible to show the level of export reduction that would be required to cause various levels of IEA supply loss. Table 34 illustrates the results.

These calculations define more precisely the impact of reductions in various OPEC subgroups' exports on the IEA's emergency reserves. Table 31 shows that a 20 percent IEA supply loss would cause the IEA to deplete 30 days' worth of oil stocks (defined according to the IEA agreement in terms of net imports) in 176 days. But using 1977 oil flows as an indicator, table 34 shows that Saudi Arabia, Kuwait, Libya, and the United Arab Emirates would have to reduce their exports to the IEA by 73 percent to bring this about. This is a far greater reduction than

Table 31
Effect of Various Levels of Oil Loss on IEA Stocks
(using 1976 data)

		Emergency Reserve Drawdown Obligation		Number of Days Required to Deplete 30-, 45-, and 60-Day Supply of Net Imports in IEA Stocks		
Percentage of Supply Loss	Percentage of Demand Restraint	Percentage of Consumption	Percentage of Imports	30	45	60
7	7	0	0	—	—	—
10	7	3	5	600	900	1,200
15	10	5	8	361	541	722
20	10	10	17	176	264	352
25	10	15	25	120	180	240
30	10	20	33	91	136	182

Note: The assumption here is that imports constitute 60 percent of IEP supplies, as they did in 1976.

they imposed in 1973. If the curtailment were a unified Arab effort, the reduction in exports would have to be 60 percent. If it were a joint OPEC effort, the reduction would have to be 36 percent.

Put another way, these calculations indicate that under the demand restraint assumptions noted previously, Saudi Arabia, Kuwait, the United Arab Emirates, and Libya would have to restrict exports to the IEA countries by 65 percent, the entire Arab group by 52 percent, and OPEC by 31 percent, to deplete 45 days' worth of net imports in IEA stocks in one year. This calculation, however, assumes that the OPEC countries provide 60 percent of the IEA group's total oil supplies. As noted in chapter 1, this situation may change in the 1980s. In particular, the Iranian oil disruptions raise the threat that the Arab countries will have a much larger share of the world export market than they had in the 1970s.

To take a pessimistic example, suppose that the IEA countries' oil consumption level in 1985 reaches 50.9 million b/d, and their import level reaches 42.2 million b/d (one of the CIA's less hopeful forecasts). This yields an import dependence of 83 percent, as compared with 60 percent in 1976. Assuming that the IEA countries have an 83 percent level of import dependence, the estimates relating oil supply losses to emergency reserve drawdowns change as shown in table 35.

Note that with each level of supply loss, it takes longer to deplete a 45-day supply of net imports in IEA members' emergency reserves (in comparison with table 31). This is because the percentage of IEA import

Table 32

OECD and IEA Oil Supplies, July 1, 1976–June 30, 1977

(in thousands of barrels per day)

Supply Sector	OECD	Non-IEA Members[a]	IEA
Indigenous Production (crude, NGL)	13,142.4	438.6	12,703.8
Imports (crude, NGL)	26,108.0	2,936.9	23,171.1
Imports (products)	5,164.4	334.9	4,829.5
Exports (crude)	1,127.2	0	1,127.2
Exports (products)	2,635.2	328.4	2,306.8
International Marine Bunkers	1,324.2	109.2	1,215.0
Total Available Supplies	39,328.2	3,272.8	36,055.4
Domestic Consumption	33,727.0	2,901.2	30,825.8

Source: Organization for Economic Cooperation and Development, *Quarterly Oil Statistics, Second Quarter 1977* (Paris: OECD, 1977).

[a] France, Finland, Iceland, and Portugal. Norway is an associate member of the IEA and is included in the IEA total.

Table 33

IEA Crude and Product Imports, July 1, 1976–June 30, 1977

(in thousands of barrels per day)

Country	Crude	Product
Algeria	777	27
Iraq	1,125	—
Kuwait	969	67
Libya	1,768	29
Qatar	253	—
Saudi Arabia	5,394	110
U.A.E.	1,510	—
Total Arab OPEC	11,796	233
Ecuador	60	—
Gabon	54	11
Indonesia	1,147	68
Iran	3,744	40
Nigeria	1,708	12
Venezuela	803	584
Total Non-Arab OPEC	7,516	715
Total OPEC	19,312	948
Norway	178	41
United Kingdom	196	273
China	133	—
U.S.S.R.	212	206
Others	2,714	3,352
Grand Total	22,745	4,820
Less IEA Exports	1,016	2,374
Net IEA Imports	21,729	2,446
Combined IEA Crude and Product Net Imports	24,175	

Source: Organization for Economic Cooperation and Development, *Quarterly Oil Statistics*, *Third Quarter 1977* (Paris: OECD, 1977).

dependence in table 35 is higher than that in table 31. The higher percentage of import dependence causes an increase in the level of IEA emergency reserves because the reserve requirement is calculated in terms of net imports. Thus, the higher the IEA percentage of dependence on oil imports, the larger the members' emergency reserves are relative to IEA oil consumption.

This increase in the group's emergency reserve level, however, is offset by the lower percentage of export curtailment required to cause a given level of IEA supply loss. In table 36, the Saudi Arabia–Kuwait–United Arab Emirate–Libya group is assumed to supply 25.3 million barrels per

Table 34
Percentage of Export Reduction Required to Cause
Various Levels of IEA Supply Loss
(using 1976 OPEC market shares)

	IEA Supply Loss		
Exporting Countries	*10%*	*20%*	*30%*
Saudi Arabia–Kuwait–U.A.E.–Libya	37	73	n.p.
Arab OPEC	30	60	90
OPEC	18	36	54

Note: n.p. = not possible.

Table 35
Effect of Various Levels of Oil Loss on IEA Stocks: Projections for the 1980s

Percentage of Supply Loss	*Percentage of Demand Restraint*	*Emergency Reserve Drawdown Obligation*		*Number of Days Required to Deplete a 45-Day Supply of Net Imports in IEA Stocks*
		Percentage of Consumption	*Percentage of Imports*	
7	7	0	0	—
10	7	3	3.75	1,245
15	10	5	6.25	747
20	10	10	12.50	374
25	10	15	18.75	249
30	10	20	25.00	187

day to the IEA countries (again, a "worst case" example, in that Saudi Arabia is assumed to produce at a level of 17.3 million b/d); OAPEC is assumed to provide 31.7 million b/d; and OPEC is assumed to provide 42.2 million b/d. In this "worst case" scenario, the level of export reductions by the two Arab groups that would be required to cause a 10, 20, and 30 percent supply loss is less than half that required in the 1976 calculations presented in table 34. The "worst case" scenario is unlikely to be realized in the 1980s, but the figures do illustrate clearly the manner in which severe oil shortages become more feasible as the oil export market becomes more concentrated.

The Politics of International Oil Crisis Management

If demand restraint of 7 or 10 percent is an unattractive response to a sudden oil loss, and emergency reserve drawdowns become increasingly

Table 36
Percentage of Export Reduction Required to Cause Various Levels
of IEA Supply Loss: Projections for the 1980s

Exporting Countries	IEA Supply Loss		
	10%	20%	30%
Saudi Arabia–Kuwait–U.A.E.–Libya	17	33	50
Arab OPEC	13	26	39
OPEC	10	20	30

unattractive, how long can cooperative international management survive? The willingness of societies to restrain demand or of governments to deplete emergency reserves is going to be influenced by individual perceptions of the level, duration, and cause of the supply problem. The reaction to an oil loss caused by an accident that is technical in nature will differ from the reaction to a loss caused by a political crisis. Governments will expect an accidental disruption to be limited in duration and will use emergency reserves in the expectations that there is no deliberate intent to weaken the nation's security.

On the other hand, a deliberate supply disruption has a completely different aspect. First, although the exporters may intend to stage only a "limited" crisis, it is unlikely that importers could afford to assume this is the case. Any deliberate disruption threatens to be open-ended.

Second, deliberate disruptions launched for political reasons may be aimed at specific countries, not at the entire group. Membership in the IEA almost automatically involves many other importers in the management of the crisis,[10] but the automaticity of the IEA "triggers" does not assure automatic unanimity on the political issue. Importers that are "hostages" in a confrontation in which they have no strong political interest are likely to be less willing to endure economic losses or to deplete their emergency reserves for the sake of the foreign policies of other importers.

Third, although the automaticity of the IEP may cause importers to *enter* the crisis collectively, at later stages the risks inherent in drawing down reserves or in continuing demand restraint may cause some importers to try to withdraw from the program. The difference in political positions that lies at the heart of the crisis may not matter in the early stages because initial drawdowns of emergency reserves may be considered "painless." But when the importers that are least committed to the political issue come to believe that the crisis will last long enough to cause a large drop in reserves, the IEP is likely to become less attractive. In effect, the emergency reserves themselves become a more valuable asset than IEA membership, and *if* there are ways to secure supplies outside the IEA framework, governments may find it less costly to drop out than to deplete their emergency reserves.

Attrition among IEA members will be most directly a function of the state of political affairs during an oil crisis. It is least likely to occur during supply disruptions that are obviously limited in duration or during disruptions in which no member country is targeted. Cooperation will be easier to maintain in these circumstances simply because the political behavior of one member is not the cause of the damage incurred by the others.

Attrition is most likely in open-ended and targeted disruptions. The key to the IEA's political cohesion in these circumstances will be the degree to which other IEA members are sympathetic toward the behavior (most likely a foreign-policy posture) of the targeted IEA member(s). Although judgments may differ over the strength of the loyalty of governments to the IEP in these circumstances, the relevant point here is that disintegrative pressures will be maximized in this scenario, and governments' willingness to use emergency reserves, or to restrain demand, cannot be taken for granted. Neither stock drawdowns nor demand restraint are cost-free.

In these most difficult political circumstances, the IEA countries may be compared to a group of labor unions united against a large industry.[11] The strike funds of the various unions may be compared to the IEA's emergency reserves. As the strike progresses, some unions are likely to deplete their strike funds before others do. As the depletion point nears, the pressure on the leaders of these unions to settle is going to increase. Three outcomes are possible. First, the poorer unions may try to reach their own settlement with industry. Second, the poorer unions may put pressure on their wealthier fellows to settle the strike more speedily. Third, the poorer unions may demand that the richer unions share their more substantial strike funds.

A similar process is likely to evolve among the IEA countries in an open-ended oil supply disruption. The countries with the smallest emergency reserves may try to reach their own accommodation with the suppliers (this seems most likely in targeted disruptions); or they may put pressure on the better-prepared importers to settle the dispute with the suppliers; or they may demand that the countries with larger stocks provide more oil, either by modifying the IEP formula or by supplying direct "subsidies" from their own emergency reserves.

The implication of this line of reasoning for the United States and Japan, the importing countries that may have the largest emergency reserves in the 1980s, is that they may not be able to enjoy unilaterally the benefits of their foresight. Like unions with large strike funds, their larger emergency reserves may cause others to impose greater responsibilities on them for the group's welfare.

Domestic and international politics are likely to influence the collective endurance of the IEA countries. This influence can be related to emergency reserve drawdowns by conducting sensitivity analyses—e.g., by varying the assumptions behind the endurance estimates of table 31.

First, assume that half the IEA countries restrain demand by only 5 percent instead of by 10 percent in a 15 percent supply reduction. Then the IEA endurance estimates presented in table 31 will change as follows:

| Percentage of Supply Loss | Percentage of Demand Restraint | Emergency Reserve Drawdown | | Number of Days Required to Deplete 45-Day Supply of Net Imports in IEA Stocks |
		Percentage of Consumption	Percentage of Imports	
15	10	5	8	541
15	5	10	17	264

The endurance level of the countries that are not willing to reduce demand by 10 percent falls to one-half that of the countries that are willing to restrain demand by that amount.

This indicates that the willingness of all IEA members to restrain demand by similar amounts is the key variable in determining the uniformity of protection provided by the present *average* IEP storage target level. In turn, the demand restraint level will indirectly influence how quickly a government will become concerned about the depletion of its reserves. Moreover, if the disruption is targeted and open-ended, the hostage countries will most likely be both unwilling to enforce rigorous demand restraint and reluctant to deplete their emergency reserves. If another way to secure additional supplies appears—e.g., if the producing countries promise to increase supplies to IEA countries that drop out of the sharing scheme—the temptation may be irresistible.

This sequence of events is not inevitable. It should be viewed as a "worst case" scenario that most vividly illustrates the interconnections between political perceptions, demand restraint, and emergency reserve drawdowns in an open-ended, targeted disruption. In a limited supply disruption, a government's decision to enforce a lower level of demand restraint has fewer political overtones. The government may do so only if it believes the crisis will not last long enough to cause a serious drop in emergency reserve levels.

The 1980s: The Defense against Oil Price Increases

One other oil problem deserves mention. The potentially tight market foreseen for the 1980s also increases the likelihood that individual oil-exporting countries will try to obtain unilateral increases in the price of their oil. In the 1970s, Saudi Arabia's shut-in production allowed it to act as a price moderator. In December 1976, for example, the Saudis and the United Arab Emirates refused to agree with their fellow OPEC members on a 10 percent oil price increase. The demand for Saudi and United Arab Emirate oil thus increased because of the lower prices, and although in June 1977 the Saudis agreed to align their prices once again with OPEC levels, the other countries agreed to freeze the price in December 1977 in light of continuing loose market conditions. The existence of spare production capacity was thus advantageous for oil consumers in two respects: it made both deliberate disruptions and price increases more difficult to implement.

It appears that the loose and hence relatively stable market of the mid-1970s gave way in 1979 to a tight market. If this market condition persists, the oil-importing countries will face a more diverse set of security problems than they worried about in the 1970s. In the loose market of the seventies, Saudi Arabia's cooperation was required to bring about an effective oil supply or price disruption. In a tight market, Saudi Arabia would (by definition) be producing all it could, having reached either the technical limits of production or a political limit set by domestic factors. In this situation, supply disruptions by "minor" producers to exact price increases from the importers would be the most salient threat to the oil-importing countries.

Given their vulnerability to sudden increases in oil prices, the oil-importing countries could decide to use their emergency reserves to deter them, and failing that, to draw stocks down in an effort to avoid immediate reliance on higher-priced oil and to cause the oil producers to lose some of their revenues. The desirability of such approaches, however, depends upon conditions that are similar to those that pertain in supply disruptions.

In evaluating the feasibility of attempts by oil-importing countries to control or influence world oil prices, the central political factor is the cohesion that exists among oil-exporting countries. In a tight market situation, attempts by importers to influence crude-oil prices by drawing down stocks may be counterproductive if the pressure on prices reflects durable changes in the supply and demand relationship. A distinction can be made between price gouging by particular oil-producing countries and a general agreement within OPEC that a price increase is in order. Several times since 1973, Saudi Arabia has opposed demands for price increases by other OPEC members. Its behavior is no doubt due to its status as a "surplus producer"—i.e., one that earns more oil revenues than are required for its immediate needs—but its power within OPEC stems from its excess oil production capacity. If its actual production level approximated the maximum technical rate, or the maximum rate that its internal politics would tolerate, its ability to restrain the price demands of other OPEC members would diminish. Consequently, even if the Saudis wanted to act as a price moderator within OPEC, they would likely need the support of several other OPEC members whose collective shut-in capacity would be sufficient to deter the price increases of other members.

In these circumstances, when OPEC itself is divided over price levels, consumers will have the best opportunity to use emergency reserve drawdowns, in conjunction with higher liftings from the moderate countries, in order to cause the price-raising exporters to lose market shares. However, if OPEC is not divided over a price increase, importers' attempts to use emergency reserve drawdowns are likely to be regarded as confrontations, and to be met by a more unified "cartel" response.

Using emergency reserves for price control purposes, even under favorable political circumstances, would be practical only under certain technical conditions. First of all, the oil in emergency reserves must correspond to the type of oil produced by the country trying to exact a price increase. Oil with a high sulfur or wax content cannot readily be used to replace oil that lacks these impurities, nor are light and heavy oils freely substitutable. Thus, if Libya were trying to increase the price of its oil, the principal Libyan customers would have to bear the brunt of the required suspension or reduction of purchases and to replace the loss with stockpile oil. Since stockpiles generally are not built up with these ends in mind—e.g., since there is not likely to be a disproportionate quantity of this particular type of crude oil in stock—the use of stocks for such price control measures could deplete the amount of Libyan oil available for future disruptions.

There is a technical solution to this problem—creating a versatile refining capability so that a wide variety of crude oils can be processed. In Japan, for example, the government is taking steps to increase the refineries' ability to handle the heavy, high-sulfur, and viscous crudes that may be more readily available in the 1980s. Due to Japan's strict environmental regulations, refiners now favor "sweet" crudes and have oriented many of their plants to process them. Thus the government must "encourage" refineries to add the desulfurization and cracking capacities to their plants to enable them to provide the required products from the presently undesirable crudes, including the quantities of oil the government has secured directly from China and Iraq.

On a global scale, however, few governments have such positive objectives for their refining industry. The high cost of modifying refineries to process many varieties of crude oil tends to make governments and oil companies rely on particular types of crudes, and hence on particular OPEC countries.

An analysis of the use of emergency reserves by importers to control the price of oil should also take into account differences in the ability of importers to use reserves for such a "nonstrategic" purpose. The ability to engage in price-control battles varies among the oil-importing countries. If it had its projected billion-barrel SPR, the United States might feel it could afford to use stocks to deal with unilateral price increases; but countries with small emergency reserves would be undermining their security against sudden supply disruptions by using their stocks as a weapon against price increases.

One other price-control option deserves mention. In 1979, the disruption in Iran's oil exports (in conjunction with several other factors too complex to describe here) caused the prices of oil sold in spot markets to escalate dramatically. OPEC responded to these events by rapidly increasing its official prices. For example, the official price of OPEC's "benchmark" crude, Saudi Arabian "Light," rose from $14 per barrel in January 1979 to $26 per barrel in January 1980. On the spot markets, Saudi "Light" sold for as much as $40 per barrel.

Many oil experts, including Walter Levy, recommended that importing countries take steps to prevent such increases in oil prices in future disruptions. Levy suggested that "a process should be designed that would discourage any country or company from paying unnecessary premiums to obtain added supplies."[12] In the International Energy Agency, discussions were held concerning the use of stock drawdowns to dampen spot-market prices.

According to government sources, the IEA deliberations have exposed many of the problems discussed in this book. Governments of countries in which emergency reserves are amalgamated with company working stocks do not know how to direct stock drawdowns so that they will have the desired effect on companies' oil-purchasing decisions. Some governments are extremely reluctant to use strategic stocks, even if they could direct them, short of a real supply emergency. Others argue that a 100 percent price increase in one year, such as occurred in 1979, *is* a real emergency. The United States is not in a strong position to lead this debate, since its strategic stock level is among the lowest in the IEA.

In short, the events of 1979 have demonstrated how ill-prepared the IEA countries are to manage oil emergencies. If the relatively minor disruption of 1979 could not be managed effectively, the prospects of managing a more severe crisis appear dim.

Conclusions

Under optimistic assumptions, the emergency stock levels of the United States, Japan, West Germany, France, Italy, and the Netherlands—when the American, German, and Japanese programs are completed—will provide substantial protection against supply losses, even if the loss is severe and countries do not restrain demand by 10 percent. *Substantial* is an ambiguous word, however. It is used here to mean that even under truly bad circumstances—a 40 percent cut in IEA exports by Arab countries in a 1980s scenario in which they control 75 percent of the export market—the IEA countries could get by for six months before some would deplete their emergency stocks. In essence, none of the six countries would suffer immediately. Reserves, coupled with a fair allocation of supplies by the IEP, would give governments time to devise a solution to the problem.

In less severe crises, stocks would also play a useful role in mitigating the effects of imperfections in the IEP allocation. Countries that were short-changed in one month could use their reserves to augment supplies, so long as the deficit was reversed in subsequent months.

This optimistic outlook for successful management of short-term or limited supply disruptions must be tempered by several caveats. First, the United States will not match the emergency reserve levels of Europe and Japan until 1983 or 1984. Until then, the United States is a weak link, a vulnerable member, in the IEP.

Second, the IEP allocation procedure has never been used. The probability of success is highly uncertain. The ability and willingness of member states to go along with the IEP's demand restraint and stock drawdown provisions are open to question. The failure of member governments to agree on a common response to the problem of oil price increases in the spot markets is sure to cause difficulties.

Finally, it is difficult to be optimistic about the ability of IEA countries to manage an open-ended crisis. A disruption caused by deliberate supply restrictions for political purposes would threaten the cohesion of the IEA on several fronts: it would raise the ugly prospect of emergency reserve depletion; provide enough time for the differences in importing countries' vulnerability to become apparent; increase the likelihood of allocation imbalances; and, being inherently political, cause "hostage" members to resent the actions of the "targets" that brought on the disruption.

9

Conclusions and Recommendations

•

The preceding chapters have presented the results of an investigation into the world oil security outlook for the 1980s. The structure of the market the oil-importing countries will be operating in is uncertain, but they have set up an emergency allocation plan for their emergency stocks. As we have seen, the oil-importing nation's stockpiling programs differ, the principal patterns being the segregated storage program of the United Unites, the combined segregated-amalgamated programs of Japan, Germany, and the Netherlands, and the amalgamated programs of France and Italy.

This investigation has also revealed that if the United States' billion-barrel plans are realized, by 1985 it will have the largest emergency reserve in proportion to net oil imports. If, in addition, U.S. imports remain below the proposed quota level of 8.2 million b/d, the SPR will provide the United States with a far greater level of protection than existing stocks will provide the other IEP countries. In short, the billion-barrel SPR would allow the United States to play a more effective role in international oil crisis management.

Analysis of the use of emergency reserves in supply disruptions necessitated a close examination of the international oil crisis management procedures of the International Energy Program. In essence, this study emphasizes that national oil supply security is a function of international factors: the depth and duration of world oil supply disruptions, the political relationships between oil-importing and oil-exporting countries, and the state of the petroleum industry. It notes that the utility of one nation's emergency reserves must be viewed in a global political and economic context because it is difficult to foresee an oil crisis that will

115

affect only one importing country. The IEP itself, plus the fact that most oil supplies are managed by international oil corporations, will internationalize oil supply crises.

The description of the emergency allocation program of the IEA covered a number of test runs, which revealed several potential issues and problems. Although many of the issues do not concern emergency reserves specifically, they are very likely to affect emergency reserve drawdowns indirectly in a real crisis. Above all, the lack of an agreement on domestic and international oil-pricing policies will make it difficult to ensure a fair allocation of supplies. This factor, coupled with the differences in national emergency reserve levels and compositions, increases the likelihood that in a crisis, some IEP members will experience oil supply problems before others do.

The book provides a manner of characterizing various types of oil supply disruptions. A distinction is made between limited and open-ended, targeted and untargeted, disruptions. These distinctions help to characterize more realistically the costs and benefits of emergency reserve drawdowns in particular situations, as well as the adequacy of emergency reserves in the IEA countries. The conclusions of this analysis are as follows:

1. Supply disruptions that governments perceive to be of *limited* duration will most likely be handled successfully by the IEP. Differences in national demand restraint and emergency reserve drawdown levels are not likely to lead to unmanagable intra-IEA tensions.

2. Untargeted, open-ended disruptions will be more difficult to manage, although the common commitment to the IEP and the availability of emergency reserves in all member countries will allow the allocation program to be used during the initial months of the crisis. Intra-IEA pressures are most likely to develop when countries with the smallest reserves begin to fear that the crisis could last long enough to cause depletion of their emergency reserves (in the sample of countries considered here, Italy is likely to be the first).

3. Targeted, open-ended disruptions will be most difficult to manage because the common commitment to the IEP is likely to be eroded by intra-IEA political differences. In these circumstances, "hostage" countries are likely to be the first to express reluctance to use emergency reserves. Drawdowns will be viewed as "penalties" incurred from association with the target countries. It is important to note that pressures on IEA cohesion are *not* likely to arise from real depletion of emergency reserves and the associated technical distribution problems that are likely to arise, but from the more fundamental resistance to using emergency reserves for a cause that is not considered worth the cost.

In short, this assessment defines the strategic context for evaluating the adequacy of emergency reserve levels within the context of the most difficult parameter of security analysis: the probability of supply disruptions.

1. The IEP—if its implementation problems can be overcome—and the *present average* emergency reserve levels are adequate defense mechanisms for limited disruptions—as much as a 20 percent IEA supply loss that is perceived will last less than a year.

2. The IEP and the present average emergency reserve level appear inadequate against extremely severe, open-ended, untargeted disruptions—e.g., a complete loss of Persian Gulf supplies. A 50 percent reduction in OPEC supplies would cause the IEA countries to deplete a 60-day supply of emergency reserves in about six months.

3. The IEP and emergency reserve levels appear least adequate to handle open-ended, targeted disruptions. However, it is argued here that the problem is structural and political; it is a problem of the kind of disruption, not the degree of preparedness. Larger stockpiles would not address the problem. Rather, the problem is political; such disruptions are not amenable to collective management.

Given these characterizations, the analytical question posed at the beginning of this book—How effective are emergency plans?—can be put in a framework of probabilities, which are neither more nor less than the hard political judgments governments must make:

1. If the probability of untargeted, open-ended disruptions is believed to be high, the average emergency reserve level should be increased.

2. If a government believes it may be a target of an open-ended disruption, it should maintain reserves that are higher than the IEA average.

How high must these probabilities be to warrant maintaining reserves above the IEA norm? A number of U.S. analysts have conducted intricate probabilistic studies linking the size of the SPR to the probability of occurrence of one or more oil supply disruptions in the 1980s. The key dimensions of deliberate and targeted disruptions, however, virtually defy rigorous analytical treatment. One such dimension is the influence the emergency reserves of *all* the IEP countries would have on the shape (level and duration) of a deliberate disruption. Most analyses describe a confrontation between only one oil-importing country (e.g., the United States) and supply disruptors, thus ignoring the fact that the IEP creates hostages that the target country cannot ignore.[1] The large U.S. SPR, for example, provides no direct insurance for Italy, Germany, and the Netherlands.

A second key dimension is the impact of the emergency reserves on the strategy of the disrupting countries. Some analysts calculate the revenue loss of the disrupting countries caused by emergency reserve drawdowns, ignoring the possibility that the disruptors would try to increase their oil prices to prevent such revenue losses. Moreover, some analysts define (and assign "expert" or "random" probabilities to) supply disruptions with fixed durations, as if emergency reserves would have no impact on the disruptors' choice of duration.[2]

Such thinking underestimates the range of options available to oil suppliers. If the oil weapon is ever used again, the disruptors' most effective coercive strategy will be defined by these kinds of assumptions. In short, to maximize their power, the disruptors should:

1. Cut exports sufficiently to cause an IEP supply loss of 15 percent or more;
2. Raise oil prices to maintain precrisis revenue levels;
3. Pick targeted countries carefully;
4. Woo "hostages" assiduously;
5. Make the crisis appear to be open-ended.

Most of the conclusions presented above are not sensitive to the inaccuracies in stockpile data. The estimated emergency reserve levels may not be accurate, but a more precise definition of emergency reserves—which could be obtained only through a more thorough assessment of oil industry operations in each country—will not change the basic uncertainty about emergency reserve use in an oil crisis. Moreover, the author's judgment is that the estimated emergency reserve levels in the countries with amalgamated programs are generous. Commercial inventory requirements are likely to be higher than the 10-day supply of crude oil and the 20-day supply of products assumed herein.

The chapters of this book have crisscrossed the paths of many diverse policy issues, from technical oil storage problems to strategic considerations. This was unavoidable, since the scope of the book is deliberately broad, the intention being to show how technical, economic, political, and strategic factors coalesce in the oil supply security problem. As a result, a long and diverse list of policy recommendations has come forth.

Recommendations for National Storage Programs

THE UNITED STATES

• The American government presently administers the Strategic Petroleum Reserve. The SPR plan should not be modified to transfer part of the emergency storage burden to the petroleum industry. As events in West Germany have shown, it is practically impossible to devise a fair storage obligation in a competitive and complex oil market.

• The Strategic Petroleum Reserve program was derailed in 1979 by the Iranian oil disruption. The 250-million-barrel target for the end of 1980 will not be met. As a result, the United States will be delayed in catching up with the emergency reserve levels of its IEA partners. The delay in acquiring SPR oil will cause the overall cost of the SPR to exceed by far the original estimates. Therefore, budget-minded officials are likely to contemplate a reduction in the billion-barrel target. If such a reassessment occurs, it would be reasonable to orient the SPR size around the reserve levels of other leading importers. For example, a 600-million-barrel SPR would give the United States a level of protection roughly similar to that of Japan. Under no circumstances, however, should SPR fill be delayed. The March 1980 deferral of SPR purchases was bad policy. It leaves the United States among the least-prepared IEA member-states.

JAPAN

• The Japanese government has embarked on an ambitious emergency storage program. Most of the Japanese emergency reserve will be amalgamated with commercial inventories. As in other amalgamated programs, the Japanese program runs the risk that, over time, emergency reserves will become more difficult to distinguish from commercial inventories as the industry gets used to operating at the higher level of stocks. In Japan, the tendency of industry to "absorb" emergency reserves can be restrained if the government provides adequate financial assistance to the oil companies to segregate their excess stocks from their commercial stocks. The lower the level of government assistance, the greater the incentive of the oil companies to treat their higher obligatory stocks as working stocks.

• The other major problem in the Japanese storage program is finding adequate space for new storage facilities. All options are being assessed, including the construction of mammoth offshore artificial storage "islands." However, such structures present a new security risk—sabotage. The existence of this threat argues for scaling down these tanks, since maximum economies of scale would expose the country to maximum losses should a mammoth structure be destroyed.

• The problem of finding sufficient storage sites also could be mitigated by lowering the storage objective. Japan may be overinsuring itself by building an American-size reserve. This book argues that most oil crises will have to be managed in such a way as to prevent depletion of the average level of IEA-country reserves; the extra insurance Japan is buying may be more than it needs, since it is unlikely to be the target of deliberate supply disruptions.

FRANCE

• The French government should consider taking measures to encourage oil companies to segregate emergency reserves from commercial inventories. It could do so by providing special financial incentives for construction of segregated emergency storage facilities.

• In addition, the emphasis on product stockpiling should be reconsidered. Since France does not import much finished product, larger crude-oil reserves are likely to provide more flexible emergency supplies than product stocks would.

ITALY

• As in the case of France, the Italian government should consider measures to encourage oil companies to segregate emergency reserves from commercial inventories.

• The storage obligation imposed on the owners of oil storage facilities (who must keep their tanks at least 20 percent full) should be eliminated. It should be replaced by a larger obligation on petroleum refiners and product importers, or by a supplemental government storage program.

• However the government chooses to augment reserves, something must be done to bring Italy up to the IEA and EEC average emergency reserve levels. While Japan may be overinsuring itself, Italy is underinsuring itself.

THE NETHERLANDS

• The emergency reserve program of the Netherlands is being reorganized as this book goes to press. The Dutch government should stick to its long-range objective of obtaining a clear-cut emergency reserve for Dutch use that is in line with the IEA and EEC average emergency reserve levels. Steps should be taken to separate the Dutch emergency reserve from the industry's working stocks (including the export working stock) to the maximum practical extent.

Recommendations Relative to the IEA's Emergency Program

• Now that IEA member countries have had several years to get their storage programs organized, the IEA Secretariat and the member governments should revise the definition of oil stocks that may be counted toward the emergency self-sufficiency reserve. As a first step, stocks in transit (in barges, intercoastal tankers, and bunkers) and storage tank bottoms should be excluded. As a second step, stocks held by "large consumers," such as electric utilities, should be excluded. As a third step, the amount of working stocks that may be included in the emergency reserve should be gradually be diminished. This suggestion assumes that the IEP members would like to move toward an eventual "real" emergency reserve of 90 days' worth of net imports. If this is not the case, it would still be useful to improve the definition in order to narrow the differences in national emergency reserve levels.

• The IEA Secretariat should conduct a study of the relationship between the mix of oils in national stockpiles and the allocation of available supplies in a crisis. Such a study may reveal, for example, that the United States needs larger product stockpiles, or that Japan will need more low-sulfur crude reserves.

• Governments should take advantage of the information that is available from previous oil supply crises and from the IEP test runs to improve their understanding of international oil flows during a crisis, and of the manner in which their actions—such as controlling domestic oil prices—affect those flows. The governments with direct control over emergency reserves—the United States, West Germany, and in the future, Japan—are particularly vulnerable to misapprehensions of international oil flows during a crisis. Their control over emergency reserves will make them a kind of "crude-rich" oil company, and their contingency planning programs must include specific policies on the level, mix, and distribution of emergency supplies to needy companies.

• Perhaps the most important neglected dimension of national and international oil crisis management is price management. In a future crisis, the lack of price policy coordination, so apparent in the 1973–74 and 1979 crises, should not be repeated. This problem has several important dimensions. For example, freezing domestic oil prices might cause oil companies to ship less oil, or lower-quality oil, than they would if prices were not frozen. As a result, the national emergency reserve would be depleted more quickly than necessary. Conversely, countries that did not freeze prices would get more supplies and would conserve their emergency reserves.

Recommendations for National Crisis Management Planning

• Many analysts tend to look at the IEA's emergency program as a "zero-sum" game, an effort that will pass or fail. In the author's opinion, it is more realistic to view the IEP as an ambitious plan to regulate an extremely complex system under difficult circumstances. It will not work perfectly, but if implemented, it will not fail completely. If it had to be implemented today, its principal difficulties would relate to the deficiency of data it receives from governments and oil companies. Its chances for success would be enhanced if the IEA Secretariat could obtain the data promptly and feel confident about their accuracy.

• IEP problems are not confined to data, however. The IEP test runs revealed that many government personnel do not understand their duties fully. National governments will be responsible for taking the actions necessary to supplement the efforts of the oil companies to achieve a fair allocation of supplies to all IEA member countries. The governments of countries that are oversupplied by oil companies will have to see to it that some supplies are diverted to the undersupplied countries. It seems that few government officials understand the difficulty and importance of fulfilling this responsibility. In addition, in many countries there appears to be an administrative gap between the officials working on the international side of oil crisis management and those working on domestic contingency plans.

• In addition, the IEA emergency program suffers from several design flaws, most of which are recognized by the Secretariat, but which are also difficult to remedy. Most important are the absence of a common emergency pricing policy and the lack of a firm agreement on demand restraint and emergency reserve drawdown levels during a crisis.

Perceptions of the Probability of Oil Supply Crises

Before 1979, oil crisis contingency planning ranked low on many governments' energy agendas. It now appears that the 1975–78 "loose" supply situation—one in which there is substantial shut-in oil production capacity—was not a permanent condition. Although oil-supply-and-demand forecasters disagree on how long 1979's "tight" market will last, the probability that it will appear again in the 1980s or 1990s is sufficiently high to justify serious preparations. If exploration in the United States' offshore areas continues to prove disappointing, if the promising new areas of supply in Mexico, China, and the North Sea are not developed to the maximum extent, if there is a war in the Middle East or prolonged civil strife in Iran, or even if there is another period of coordinated rapid economic growth in the OECD countries, the excellence of countries' contingency plans and the ready availability of emergency reserves will be crucial factors in the economic and political well-being of oil-importing countries.

Analysis of National Emergency Reserve Levels

•

To derive rough estimates of the amount of oil in company stocks that could be considered emergency reserves, it is necessary to take into account the operating requirements of the oil industry. Companies that refine and market oil need to keep substantial stocks on hand. How much oil they need to hold, however, is difficult to determine. Essentially, stocks are needed to smooth out "bumps" in petroleum deliveries. Moreover, since many refineries process more than one type of crude oil, and types need to be segregated until they are mixed in specific proportions, tanks to hold each crude type must be available.

The situation is more complicated for refineries that rely on foreign crude shipped to them in tankers. A 100,000-ton shipment, or 700,000 barrels, represents about a 5-day supply of crude for a typical large refinery. Since many of these refineries run various crude types, they must be prepared to hold one type for several days before it can be blended with another type. In addition, import-dependent refiners must protect themselves from disrupted shipping schedules. To provide a rather modest coverage for the likelihood that a crude-oil tanker will be delayed, a refinery may plan on a possible 20 percent delay in an average tanker voyage (30 days), which would require holding an additional 6-day supply of the various crudes in stock. Thus, a coastal refinery needs to maintain about a 10-day supply of crudes in stock.

CRUDE-OIL STOCKS

Tables A-1 and A-2 provide average annual crude stock levels in millions of barrels and days' worth of average refinery throughput in each country from 1973 to 1978. Figure A-1, which is drawn from monthly stock level data, provides a clearer indication of the seasonal movement of crude-oil stocks.

Figure A-1 helps to flesh out the averages presented in table A-1. The data for the United States, Japan, and Germany all indicate a gradual increase in crude-oil stocks. The German and Japanese increases can be attributed to the impact of the higher national storage targets imposed in both countries in 1975. In Germany, the increases also are due to the build-up of the Federal Reserve, which at the end of 1978 comprised more than one-third of the total national crude stockpile. The steady increases in crude stocks in Germany and Japan also suggest that the oil companies tend to put increases in obligatory levels into crude rather than product stocks.[1]

The increase in U.S. crude stocks cannot be credited to government storage regulations, because the governmnet has not imposed any; nor is the increase the result of the build-up of the Strategic Reserve (which contained 66 million barrels at the end of 1978), because SPR stocks are reported separately. Closer examination of the statistics on U.S. crude reveals that the increase is due to the build-up of stocks of foreign crudes and the increase in production of Alaskan oil (operation of the Alaskan pipeline appears to require up to 15 million barrels of working stocks).[2]

The changes in the French, Italian, and Dutch stocks are too erratic to suggest a trend. For France, the absence of a gradual increase is not surprising, since its storage regulations did not change in the years 1973–78. The Italian government, on the other hand, did increase its national storage target from 70 to 90 days in 1976. The fact that this change is not evident in figure A-1 can be attributed to several factors. First, the data is for end-of-quarter stock levels only, and thus may provide an inaccurate picture of average month-end stock levels. The extreme drop in Italian stocks in March 1977 may be more of an aberration than the data suggest.[3] Second, it may be that the new regulations were applied or interpreted so as to have a larger impact on the stock levels of non-oil industry owners of crude than on the refiners. Third, the largest part of the refiners' stock increase may have been passed on to product stocks. In the Netherlands, the government imposed a 90-day obligation in 1976, but the regulation had no practical effect on stock levels, because the oil industry already held far more than the equivalent of 90 days of Dutch domestic sales in order to conduct its extensive export operations.

To estimate the size of the total crude-oil stockpile that can be considered an emergency reserve in each country, it will be assumed that a 10-day supply of average refinery throughput is needed to provide

Figure A-1
Month-End Crude-Oil Stocks, January 1973–June 1979

Only end-of-quarter data are available for Italy after 1973. Figures for 1978 and
March 1979 are unavailable for Italy and the Netherlands; OECD quarterly
figures are used.

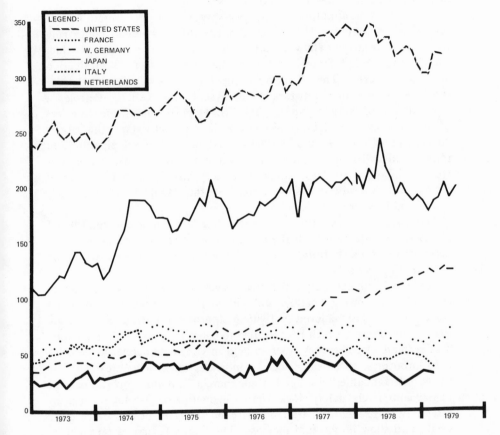

each refinery with the proper quantities and mix of crude-oil types.
This would mean that at any given time, a number of refineries would
have a 5-day supply in stock, and a number would have a 15-day supply.
This is necessarily an arbitrary estimate of minimum commercial-crude
stock requirements. If anything, it is too low—i.e., it is not likely that
all refineries could be supplied with their preferred mix of crudes at
this average level. The guess that a 10-day supply might not be sufficient to allow all countries to be resupplied with crude oil in time to
prevent particular refineries from running out is based on the OECD
group's average crude stock level. According to OECD quarterly oil

statistics, this level fluctuates between 25 and 33 days, worth of average total OECD refinery throughput from 1973 to 1978.[4] Thus, the assumption that the refineries need a minimum working stock of crude equivalent to 10 days of average throughput presupposes that they could operate at one-third the normal level of crude stocks.[5]

Within this assumption, it is necessary to consider some factors related to the data on U.S. stocks. A specific problem in comparing the American stock data with other stock data derives from the fact that in the United States, extensive pipelines connect oil production areas to refineries. The oil used for pipeline fill is not deducted from the national stockpile statistics. An analysis by the National Petroleum Council (an advisory group to the U.S. Department of the Interior) of the emergency availability of commercial oil stocks states that about 30 percent of reported crude stocks must be considered pipeline and refinery fill and tank bottoms.[6] This amount, along with the working-stock estimate of 10 days, worth of refinery inputs, must be deducted from total U.S. crude stocks to approximate the actual level of emergency reserves in U.S. crude-oil stocks.

The statistics of the other countries already exclude pipeline-fill oil. A 5 percent deduction from the average stock levels of crude—made to account for tank bottoms—yields the emergency reserves of crude estimated in Table A-3.

Table A-3 indicates that the stock levels of German and Japanese crude oil are growing steadily, and will continue to grow until national storage targets are achieved in 1980. Also growing is the U.S. Strategic Petroleum Reserve, which is scheduled to contain up to 1 billion barrels. The estimate of emergency reserves held in U.S. commercial inventories is so uniform as to be suspicious; it indicates more of a "steady state" in the oil companies' unimpeded commercial inventory operations, an 11-day commercial safety stock, than a deliberate or growing emergency reserve. The French and Italian emergency reserves of crude are quite small, and show no gradual increase. The Dutch reserve is fattened by export stocks.

PRODUCT STOCKS

Tables A-4 and A-5 provide yearly averages of combined gasoline, distillate, and residual-fuel-oil stocks for the years 1973–78.

As with crude-oil statistics, the totals in table A-4 do not indicate the volume of emergency reserves in product stockpiles. Estimates of the emergency reserve levels in these stocks must account for the differences between crude-oil and finished-product distribution systems. In each country crude stocks are held principally at refineries for processing there.[7] Products, on the other hand, extend into the market; product stocks are held by refineries, bulk terminals, and wholesalers and retailers (whose stocks are not included in the statistics). Typically, the refinery produces a number of distinct finished products and stores them separately. Its distributors periodically "raid" these stocks and move lumps of products via coastal tankers, barges, or tank trucks to their own storage tanks, which in turn are tapped by retailers. Thus, there are, in a sense, two commercial inventories in the product distribution system: that of the refinery and that of the distributor. The same structure exists in the crude-oil distribution system, of course, but the commercial inventory of the *refinery's* supplier (i.e., the tank farms of the oil-producing countries) cannot be counted as part of the importing country's stocks.

The two commercial inventories in the product distribution system make it even more difficult to estimate the minimum supply level required to sustain smooth operations. The U.S. oil industry has kept the equivalent of 30-40 days of demand in "unavailable" *and* cycle stocks over the last four years. European and Japanese refiners, however, have less extensive pipeline systems and thus need to maintain a lower level of "unavailable" stocks.

In the following breakdowns of product stocks, it will be assumed that companies need to maintain the equivalent of about 20 days of average inland demand for cycle stocks in their gasoline and distillate distribution systems, and about 10 days of demand for residual oil. The lower figure for residual oil reflects the rather limited market of a small number of customers using large quantities of residual fuel.

Seasonal fluctuations in demand have the greatest effect on the management of distillate- and residual-oil stocks. In the discussion of these product stocks, the high and low yearly stock levels are compared to determine seasonal stock adjustment. This figure indicates how much of the total stockpile is delegated to meeting demand while demand exceeds production capacity, and therefore cannot be depended on for emergency use.

Trading stocks comprise an important segment of the product stockpiles of Italy and the Netherlands; 15 percent of Italian finished products and 70 percent of Dutch finished products are exported or sold as international marine bunkers. The export stocks pose a particular problem for the Netherlands. When the Dutch government and oil industry began discussing the establishment of a Central Storage Organization (CSO) that would hold part of the Dutch emergency reserve, their discussions focused on the specific working-stock requirement for the oil industry's *export* working stocks. A tentative figure of 32 days' worth of average exports (including bunkers) has been agreed upon for the purpose of establishing the interim CSO. The 32-day working-stock deduction is an attempt to classify Dutch stocks in terms of their availability to the Dutch market during supply difficulties. It should not be considered an accurate accounting of the stocks dedicated to exports and bunkers. These are about 70 percent of total refinery output, and it is likely that about 70 percent of total stocks normally are held for ultimate delivery to foreign customers. The "32-day" provision covers only 30 percent of the total as export stocks. When the supply situation becomes "abnormal," however, some of the export stocks not included in the "32-day" figure probably could be used to offset Dutch oil losses.[8]

On the basis of these general observations, the emergency reserves in product stocks can be assessed by examining gasoline, distillate, and residual fuel oil separately.

GASOLINE

Tables A-6 and A-7 list the average gasoline stocks held by the six countries surveyed for the years 1973–78. Figure A-2, which is based on monthly stock statistics, illuastrates the seasonal fluctuations in stocks.

Figure A-2 indicateṣ that gasoline stocks in the Unites States and Germany remained relatively stable during this period, showing neither a general increase in stock levels (in contrast to crude-oil stocks) nor substantial seasonal fluctuations.

In the case of Japan, the graph indicates a regular pattern: stocks peak in early summer and reach a trough at the end of each year. A seasonal stock of about 3 million barrels is built in the spring to prepare for summer demand surges. In France, the seasonal build-up averages 5 million barrels.

Italy shows an inconsistent variation: gasoline stocks peaked in December 1973, March 1974, December 1975, and December 1976, and then zoomed up in March 1977, the same month in which stocks of Italian crude oil plummeted. The March 1977 increase may indicate the Italian oil companies' reaction to the onset of the 1976 rules: they may have found it more economical to "top off" gasoline stocks. Given the higher cost of gasoline storage, this does not seem likely; thus, the coincidental drop in crude stocks and increase in gasoline stocks may be only a statistical coincidence. The quarterly data are not adequate to make a judgment. However, one can make some inferences about the influence of Italian gasoline exports on gasoline stocks. Expressing the December 1976 stock level—12.7 million barrels—in days of 1976 domestic gasoline sales yields a 50-day stock; making the same calcula-

Figure A-2
Month-End Gasoline Stocks, January 1973–June 1979

France (the CPP) did not provide a full count of gasoline stocks before January 1974.
Only end-of-quarter data are available for Italy after 1973. Figures for 1978 and
March 1979 are unavailable for Italy and the Netherlands; OECD quarterly
figures are used.

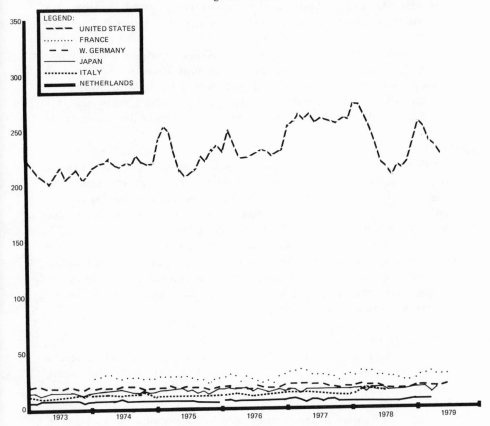

tion in days of average 1976 domestic sales plus exports yields only a
37-day stock. One must take into account, however, that some gasoline
goes to spot markets rather than to "regular customers," and during
a supply crisis, Italian companies might retain the amounts that normally
go to the spot markets in order to sustain their exports to regular
customers. Italian export statistics indicate that certain European and
African countries consistently receive 50 percent of Italy's gasoline

exports. Thus, assuming that Italy will sustain these exports during a crisis, a 20-day supply of "regular exports" will be added to the commercial inventories estimated below. A similar situation exists in the Netherlands, which regularly ships about 50,000 barrels a day to Germany, Belgium, and other European countries.

Tables A-8, A-9, and A-10 provide estimates of gasoline emergency reserves. The United States and Germany are grouped in table A-8 because their gasoline stocks show little seasonal fluctuation and because they do not need to maintain export stocks. Table A-9 groups Japan and France because their stocks show distinct seasonal fluctuations. Table A-10 groups Italy and the Netherlands because they need to maintain export working stocks. In all three tables, the equivalent of 20 days of average demand, as expressed in inland sales data for gasoline, is deducted from total stocks to account for commercial inventory requirements.

The emergency reserve estimates show that the United States and Japan have insubstantial emergency gasoline reserves. Germany's figure is somewhat higher, but shows none of the steady growth that is so visible in its crude-oil stockpile. Thus, as in the case of Japan, the estimates suggest that German companies prefer not to stockpile gasoline to meet the higher storage obligations imposed in 1975.

The Italian and Dutch gasoline emergency reserve estimates are even more substantial than Germany's, but in both cases export business complicates the estimate. France's gasoline emergency reserve is the largest, reflecting the emphasis of French storage regulations on product rather than crude-oil stockpiling.

DISTILLATE OILS

Tables A-11 and A-12 provide yearly averages of distillate stocks for the years 1973-78. Figure A-3, which is based on monthly stock statistics, illustrates the pronounced seasonal fluctuations that occur in these stocks.

Table A-12 shows a large discrepancy in distillate-oil stocks between France and the Netherlands—which have about a 100-day supply in stock on the average—and the other four countries. The level of Dutch stocks can again be explained by the existence of export stocks. The French average, however, does indicate a deliberately large distillate stock resulting from product-oriented storage regulations.

It is important to observe that French distillate stocks experience unusually large seasonal stock build-ups in comparison with the seasonal fluctuations that occur in the other five countries. These seasonal stocks must be taken into account in estimating emergency reserve levels. This is done by taking the difference in each year's high and low stock

Figure A-3
Month-End Distillate-Oil Stocks, January 1973–June 1979

Japan's figures include both kerosene and gas-oil. Japan's figures for February–June 1978
are unavailable; OECD figures are used. France (the CPP) did not provide a full count
of distillate stocks before January 1974. Only end-of-quarter data are available for
Italy after 1973. Figures for 1978 and March 1979 are unavailable for Italy and the
Netherlands; OECD quarterly figures are used.

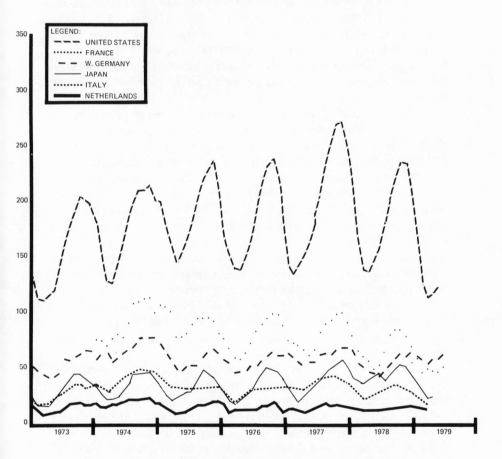

levels and calculating an average seasonal build-up. Thus, France's
average seasonal build-up is 36 million barrels, the United States' is
90 million barrels, Japan's is 23 million barrels, and Germany's is 19
million barrels.

In Italy, the distillate market is complicated by exports. Since 1973,
about 70 percent of Italy's distillate exports have gone to France,
Switzerland, Germany, and Africa. The level of these exports, how-

ever, declined from an average of 154,000 b/d in 1973 to 116,000 b/d in 1975 and 86,000 b/d in 1976. The average then rose slightly to 99,000 b/d in 1977. The amount of working stocks needed for export has declined. In addition, and perhaps due to inadequate data, the seasonal build-up seems to be less consistent in Italy than it is elsewhere: 4.7 million barrels in 1973, 15.6 million barrels in 1974, 12.1 million barrels in 1975, only 4 million barrels in 1976, and back to 12.4 million barrels in 1977, or a rather tenuous "average" of 9 million barrels.

The Dutch distillate market also is complicated by a high export level. Dutch refineries export about 250,000 b/d, mostly to Germany. Both exports and domestic sales fluctuate seasonally, and stocks are built up by about 8 million barrels each year to meet winter demand surges.

Tables A-13 and A-14 provide estimates of emergency reserves of distillate oil at the highest and lowest levels of the distillate stock cycle. Table A-13 groups the United States, Japan, Germany, and France; deducts the equivalent of 20 days of average demand from total stocks to reflect the commercial inventory; and deducts the average seasonal build-up from the high stock level. Table A-14 groups Italy and the Netherlands to illustrate the effects of the export-working-stock requirements on emergency reserve estimates.

These tables are almost too dense to be editorially acceptable. Yet their complexity helps make the point that distillate stocks, which constitute up to one-half of the average national oil stockpile in some countries, and more than that during September and October, must not be regarded as an inert quantity of oil whose use in a crisis would be a simple matter. Large stockpiles of distillate exist in most countries because refineries cannot produce enough of the fuel during the winter months.

Given this cautionary note, the tables can be taken to indicate that the seasonally adjusted emergency reserves of distillate oils are relatively small compared to present (or anticipated) emergency crude-oil reserves in the Unites States, Japan, and Germany. Once again, the emergency reserve levels in the Netherlands and in Italy are contingent on assumptions about exports. And France's reserve, again reflecting the emphasis of government regulations on finished-product rather than crude-oil stockpiling, is the most substantial.

RESIDUAL FUEL OIL

Tables A-15 and A-16 provide average yearly residual-oil stock levels for the years 1973–78. Figure A-4 is based on monthly stock data.

Table A-16 shows that the Netherlands and France have the largest stocks of residual oil in terms of the number of days of inland sales.

Figure A-4
Month-End Residual-Oil Stocks, January 1973–June 1979

France (the CPP) did not provide a full count of residual-fuel stocks before January 1974. Only end-of-quarter data are available for Italy after 1973. Figures for 1978 and March 1979 are unavailable for Italy and the Netherlands; OECD quarterly figures are used.

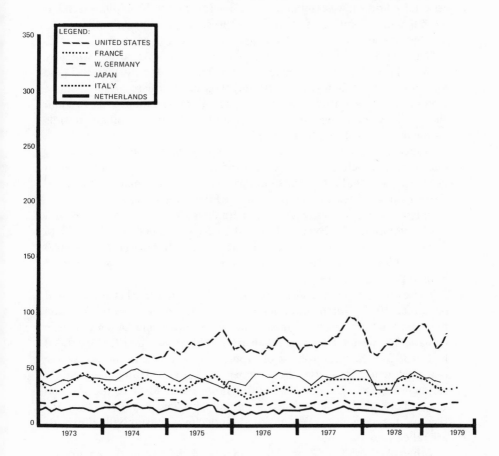

Once again, this is due to the existence of export stocks in the Netherlands and to the French government's emphasis on product stockpiling.

There are distinct seasonal fluctuations in the stock levels of residual fuel oil in each country. In the United States, the seasonal swings are obscured by a general increase in stocks of residual fuel oil. This is due to a slow increase in the production of residual oil by U.S. refiners and a corresponding decrease in imports of residual oil, which provided 66 percent of U.S. supplies of residual oil in 1973, but 42 percent in 1977. Within this general swing toward decreased dependence on imports, seasonal fluctuations have averaged about 16 million barrels since 1973.

Japan's imports of residual fuel oil also have declined: from 230,000 b/d in 1973 to 158,000 b/d in 1977. Somewhat suprisingly, however, the average stock level has not changed significantly. Japan's stocks of residual oil do show seasonal fluctuations (averaging 10 million barrels), although in the spring of 1975, stocks were at an unusually high level, making the normal summer build-up unnecessary.

Germany imports only about 15 percent of its residual oil, which is a much lower import percentage than is required for distillates. These low stocks of residual oil suggest that German refiners prefer to meet their stockpiling obligations with crude oil rather than with residual stocks. This is evident also in the small build-up—7 million barrels on the average—of seasonal stocks.

France's residual stocks are considerably larger than Germany's, due to the French government's restrictions on the use of crude oil to meet the residual-oil storage obligation. The seasonal build-up of French stocks of residual oil has averaged 9 million barrels.

Italy's market for residual oil is complicated by its falling export and rising import levels. Exports have fallen from 195,000 b/d in 1973 to 78,000 b/d in 1977; in the same period, imports have risen from 49,000 b/d to 100,000 b/d. The seasonal build-up in stocks has averaged 12 million barrels since 1973.

The export factor is also important in the Dutch market for residual oil. Since 1973, Dutch refineries have exported or sold as bunker fuel more than 80 percent of their residual-oil output, while Dutch domestic demand for residual oil had fallen from 90,000 b/d in 1973 to 60,000 b/d in 1976. The large volume of exports, combined with the decreasing domestic demand, cause the number of days of Dutch demand in residual stocks to balloon, as seen in table A-16. Most of the residual stocks held in the Netherlands eventually become exports. Thus, the size of emergency reserves of residual oil declines substantially if exports are taken into account.

Tables A-17 and A-18 provide estimates of the size of the emergency reserves of residual fuel oil at the highest and lowest points in the stock cycle. Table A-17 groups the countries that do not export large quantities of residual fuel. Table A-18 groups Italy and the Netherlands to illustrate the effects of export working stocks on emergency reserve estimates. In both tables, commercial stock levels include both domestic sales and bunker fuel sales on the grounds that demand for bunker fuel will have to be met in an oil crisis.

The tables indicate that stockpiles of residual oil in the United States and Japan contain relatively small emergency reserves, the equivalent of less than 20 days of the previous year's average sales of residual oil. The German and French figures are somewhat higher, with the French approximating 40 days of residual sales. The Italian reserve is in the same range, and unlike the situation with regard to distillate stocks, has scarcely been affected by export volumes. The same cannot be said for the Netherlands, although even after deducting the "export working stock," the Dutch have the equivalent of more than 100 days of domestic residual oil sales in their emergency reserve. This phenomenon can be attributed to a small divisor: the demand for residual oil in the Netherlands fell sharply, from nearly 90,000 b/d in 1973 to 38,000 b/d in 1975, and then rose slightly to 45,000 b/d in 1977.

SUMMARY

In table A-19 the estimated emergency reserve volumes in product stockpiles are listed for the years 1973–78 for the United States, Japan, Germany, France, Italy, and the Netherlands.

To transform the volumetric estimates of emergency reserves of the principal finished products cited in table A-19 and the reserves of crude oil given in table A-3 into a more useful comparative form, table A-20 lists the emergency reserves in terms of the equivalent number of days of net imports during the previous year. The net import data used in this calculation are given in table A-21.

NOTE ON SOURCES OF STOCKPILE DATA

At present, there are two publications that provide information on the oil stock levels of OECD countries. One is the "Statistical Survey" from the biweekly *International Oil Developments,* published by the U.S. Central Intelligence Agency (but only the "Statistical Survey" is unclassified and available to the public).[9] This publication provides month-end stock data for the United States, Japan, Canada, Austria, Belgium, Denmark, France, Ireland, and Italy. This source was not used for this study, because it does not distinguish between crude and product stocks, and because it does not include Germany and the Netherlands.

The second source is the OECD/IEA publication *Quarterly Oil Statistics,* a new series that replaces the OECD's *Provisional Oil Statistics by Quarter,* providing more extensive statistical coverage than its predecessor. One of the valuable features of the new report is that it provides end-of-quarter data on stocks of crude oil, natural-gas liquids, feed-stocks and finished products (gasoline, naphtha, liquid-petroleum gases, gasoline, kerosene, jet fuel, distillate oil or gas/diesel oil, and residual fuel oil are listed separately). This source was not used for this study, however, because monthly data were required, and because the series begins with 1975, and figures for 1973–74 were needed.

Since these two sources did not provide satisfactory data, it was necessary to seek out the best available data for each country separately, as noted below. The statistical bases for each country's reported stock levels are not identical.

1. U.S. stock, import, and domestic sales statistics were taken from the U.S. Bureau of Mines' "Monthly Petroleum Statement," 1973 through 1976. (In January 1975, the Bureau first included stocks from approximately 100 bulk terminals. This added about 45 million barrels to the totals reported on the previous basis). Data for 1977 and 1978 were taken from the Department of Energy's *Monthly Energy Review.*

2. German oil company stock statistics were provided by the Arbeitsgemeinschaft Erdöl-Gewinnung und-Verarbeitung (AEV), an industry association. Government crude stock data were provided by the Bundesministerium für Wirtschaft, Bonn.

3. French stock statistics were taken from the *Bulletin Mensuel,* a publication of the Comité Professionnel du Petrole, Paris.

4. Italian stock statistics were provided by Ente Nazionale Idrocarburi (ENI), the state-owned oil company, Rome.

5. Dutch stock statistics were provided by the Ministerie van Economische Zaken, The Hague.

6. Japanese stock, import, and domestic sales data were provided by the Petroleum Association of Japan, Tokyo.

The stock data are not based on uniform reporting techniques. For example, the technical specifications of finished products differ somewhat from country to country: the term *distillate fuels* does not mean exactly the same type of fuel when translated into the German *Distillat-Heizöle* and the French *Gas-oil et fuel-oil fluides.*[10]

However, these data drawbacks need not cripple the kind of analysis performed in this study. For the purposes of this report, it is sufficient to determine roughly the magnitude of stocks and the division between crude-oil and finished-product stocks. Therefore, the data in the preceding graphs are presented with the assurance that they are the best data readily available to one willing to seek out national sources of information. They are, in every instance, the data used by governments in their reports to the public and to the OECD/IEA.

TABLE A-1

Average Month-end Crude Oil Stocks

(in millions of barrels)

	1973	1974	1975	1976	1977	1978
USA: Oil company stocks	245	260	272	286	324	330
Strategic reserve	0	0	0	0	8	66
Japan: Oil company stocks	121.7	160.5	179.3	180.8	200.0	205
JNOC strategic reserve	-	-	-	-	-	44
Germany: Total average stocks	39.3	46.3	57.6	78.1	96.5	108
of which Federal reserve	0	3.0	12.0	26.0	33.0	48
France	54.2	66.4	70.1	62.8	68.7	60.0
Italy	51.9	62.3	60.2	56.6	48.5	47
The Netherlands	26.4	33.9	38.9	35.6	37.7	29

TABLE A-2

Average Month-end Crude Oil Stocks

(in days of average refinery throughput)

	1973	1974	1975	1976	1977	1978
USA: Oil company stocks	20	21	21	21	22	21
Strategic reserve	0	0	0	0	0.5	4
Japan: Oil company stocks	28	37	44	43	46	41
JNOC strategic reserve	-	-	-	-	-	9
Germany: Total average stocks	16	21	30	37	48	45
of which: Federal reserve	0	1	6	12	16	15
France	20	25	32	26	29	29
Italy	20	26	29	26	22	21
The Netherlands	19	26	34	27	31	33

APPENDIX

TABLE A-3

Estimated Emergency Reserves of Crude Oil

(in millions of barrels)

	1973	1974	1975	1976	1977	1978
U.S.A.						
Average crude stocks*	245	260	272	286	324	330
Commercial inventories	125	121	129	138	147	158
Pipeline fill/tank bottoms[1]	74	78	82	86	97	99
Emergency reserves	46	61	61	62	80	73
In days of previous year's net imports	11	11	11	11	11	9
Japan						
Average crude stocks	121.7	160.5	179.3	180.8	200.0	249
Commercial inventories	44.3	43.0	40.5	42.2	43.5	42.4
Tank bottoms	6.1	8.0	9.0	9.0	10.0	11.0
Emergency reserves	71.3	109.5	129.8	129.6	146.5	195.6
In days of previous year's net imports	17	23	27	29	31	39
Germany						
Average crude stocks**	39.3	46.3	57.6	78.1	96.5	108.0
Commercial inventories	23.7	21.6	18.9	20.6	20.1	21.6
Tank bottoms***	2.0	2.2	2.3	2.6	3.2	3.0
Emergency reserves	13.7	22.6	36.4	54.9	73.2	83.4
In days of previous year's net imports	6	8	14	23	27	32
France						
Average crude stocks	54.2	66.4	70.1	62.8	68.7	60.0
Commercial inventories	27.1	26.7	21.8	24.4	23.7	23.6
Tank bottoms	2.7	3.3	3.5	3.1	3.4	3.0
Emergency reserves	24.4	36.4	44.8	38.4	41.6	33.4
In days of previous year's net imports	9	14	20	14	20	16
Italy						
Average crude stocks	51.9	62.3	60.2	56.6	48.5	47.0
Commercial inventories	25.8	24.0	20.4	21.9	22.0	23.1
Tank bottoms	2.6	3.1	3.0	2.8	2.4	2.4
Emergency reserves	23.5	35.2	36.8	31.9	24.1	21.5
In days of previous year's net imports	13	18	18	18	13	12
The Netherlands						
Average crude stocks	26.4	33.9	38.9	35.6	37.7	29.0
Commercial inventories	14.3	12.7	11.0	13.0	12.1	11.6
Tank bottoms	1.3	1.7	2.0	1.8	1.9	1.5
Emergency reserves	10.8	19.5	25.9	20.8	23.7	15.9
In days of previous year's net imports	20	35	49	50	45	38

*   Excluding the Strategic Reserve

** Including the Federal Reserve

***Excluding the Federal Reserve

NOTES TO TABLE A-3

1. This figure is assumed to be 30 percent of the total crude stocks reported. The National Petroleum Council's Petroleum Storage Capacity
   report (September 1974), which contains an analysis of the emergency
   availability of U.S. commercial inventories, states that about 30
   percent of reported crude oil stocks must be considered pipeline and
   refinery fill and tank bottoms.

   For the other countries, tank bottoms are assumed to be 5 percent of
   the average stock level.

TABLE A-4

Average Principal Petroleum Product Stocks

(in millions of barrels)

	1973	1974	1975	1976	1977	1978
USA	415	450	489	484	536	497
Japan	82	94	87	92	96	94
Germany	93	105	96	90	98	90
France	n.a.	151	146	135	138	128
Italy	75	87	77	66	93	82
The Netherlands	33	39	33	31	33	30

NOTE: Includes gasoline, distillate and residual fuel oil.

TABLE A-5

Average Principal Petroleum Product Stocks

(in days of domestic sales)

	1973	1974	1975	1976	1977	1978
USA	33	37	41	39	39	37
Japan	24	28	28	29	28	28
Germany	41	53	48	44	45	43
France	n.a.	87	91	76	81	77
Italy	55	63	57	48	65	63
The Netherlands	103	150	127	111	120	108

APPENDIX

TABLE A-6

Average Gasoline Stocks

(in millions of barrels)

	1973	1974	1975	1976	1977	1978
USA	210	220	228	230	258	235
Japan	13.4	14.5	15.0	15.6	15.3	15.3
Germany	18.3	17.8	17.6	17.6	19.2	17.5
France	n.a.	27.1	26.3	25.7	29.3	27.5
Italy	10.2	12.1	10.4	11.4	17.8	16.0
The Netherlands	5.7	6.0	5.6	5.8	6.2	5.3

TABLE A-7

Average Gasoline Stocks

(in days of average domestic gasoline sales)

	1973	1974	1975	1976	1977	1978
USA	31	33	34	33	36	31
Japan	29	32	30	30	28	27
Germany	43	42	38	37	38	32
France	n.a.	79	72	66	73	67
Italy	39	49	40	45	72	60
The Netherlands	71	80	70	77	68	70

TABLE A-8

Estimated Emergency Gasoline
Reserves in the U.S. and in Germany

(in millions of barrels)

	1973	1974	1975	1976	1977	1978
1. U.S.A.						
Average stock level	210	220	228	230	258	235
Pipeline fill[1]	36	37	39	39	44	40
Commercial inventories	133	131	133	140	144	150
Emergency reserves:						
volume	41	52	56	51	70	45
in days of previous						
year's demand	6	8	9	8	10	6
2. GERMANY						
Average stock level	19	18	18	18	19	18
Commercial inventories	9	9	9	10	10	11
Emergency reserves:						
volume	10	9	9	8	9	7
in days of previous						
year's demand	22	20	20	18	19	13

[1]Figures represent 17 percent of total stocks, using the National
Petroleum Council's analysis of March 1973 and September 1973 stocks.

APPENDIX

TABLE A-9

Marked Seasonal Fluctuations:
Estimated Emergency Gasoline Reserves
in Japan and in France

(in millions of barrels)

	1973 High	1973 Low	1974 High	1974 Low	1975 High	1975 Low	1976 High	1976 Low	1977 High	1977 Low	1978 High	1978 Low
1. JAPAN												
Stock level	14	12	16	13	16	13	18	15	16	15	16	14
Commercial inventories	9	9	9	9	10	10	11	11	11	11	11	11
Seasonal stock	3	0	3	0	3	0	3	0	3	0	3	0
Emergency reserves:												
volume	2	3	4	4	3	3	4	4	2	4	1	3
in days of previous year's demand	5	7	8	8	6	6	8	8	4	8	2	6
2. FRANCE												
Stock level	n.a.	n.a.	30	26	28	23	28	22	33	24	32	24
Commercial inventories	n.a.	n.a.	7	7	7	7	8	8	8	8	8	8
Seasonal stock	n.a.	n.a.	5	0	5	0	5	0	5	0	5	0
Emergency reserves:												
volume	n.a.	n.a.	18	19	16	16	15	14	20	16	19	16
in days of previous year's demand	n.a.	n.a.	49	52	45	45	42	38	51	41	48	40

TABLE A-10

The Trade Factor:
Estimated Emergency Gasoline Reserves
In Italy and in the Netherlands

(in millions of barrels)

	1973	1974	1975	1976	1977	1978
1. ITALY						
Average stock level	10	12	10	11	18	16
Commercial inventories						
a) domestic sales only	5	5	5	5	5	5
b) including regular exports	6	6	6	6	6	8
Emergency reserves: volumes						
a) without export working stocks	5	7	5	6	13	11
b) with export working stocks	4	6	4	5	7	8
Emergency reserves: days of previous year's inland sales						
a) without export working stocks	21	28	22	24	51	44
b) with export working stock	18	24	19	21	28	32
2. NETHERLANDS						
Average stock level	6	6	6	6	6	5
Commercial inventories						
a) domestic sales only	2	2	2	2	2	2
b) including regular exports	3	3	3	3	3	5
Emergency reserves: volumes						
a) without export working stocks	4	4	4	4	4	3
b) with export working stocks	3	3	3	3	3	0
Emergency reserves: days of previous year's inland sales						
a) without export working stocks	52	55	55	53	46	30
b) with export working stocks	39	39	38	38	34	0

APPENDIX

TABLE A-11

Average Distillate Oil Stocks

(in millions of barrels)

	1973	1974	1975	1976	1977	1978
U.S.A.	155.0	175.0	189.0	184.0	199.0	186.0
Japan	29.0	34.6	32.9	34.0	38.1	45.3
Germany	53.0	56.0	57.7	54.4	60.0	54.8
France	n.a.	90.1	88.5	78.5	79.9	68.0
Italy	25.9	41.1	31.4	27.9	36.2	28.0
The Netherlands	13.7	18.9	14.7	13.9	13.6	13.0

NOTE: Gasoil and kerosene are included in Japan's figures.

TABLE A-12

Average Distillate Oil Stocks

(in days of average domestic sales)

	1973	1974	1975	1976	1977	1978
U.S.A.	50	60	68	59	60	55
Japan	44	54	51	49	53	58
Germany	41	50	51	44	48	42
France	n.a.	117	120	102	103	80
Italy	71	105	78	61	80	57
The Netherlands	91	151	113	96	97	86

TABLE A-13

Estimated Emergency Distillate Reserves in
the Four Nonexporting Countries

(in millions of barrels)

	1973		1974		1975		1976		1977		1978	
	High	Low	High	Low	High	Low	High	Low	High	Low	High	Low
1. U.S.A.												
Stock level	203	111	213	125	235	146	236	137	270	133	233	136
Pipeline fill[1]	20	11	21	13	24	15	24	14	27	13	23	13
Commercial inventories	62	62	58	58	56	56	62	62	66	66	68	68
Seasonal Stock	90	0	90	0	90	0	90	0	90	0	90	0
Emergency reserves: volume	31	38	44	54	65	75	60	61	87	54	52	55
in days of previous year's demand	10	13	14	18	22	26	21	21	28	17	16	17
2. JAPAN												
Stock level	44	16	46	22	43	22	48	21	56	21	52	22
Commercial inventories	13	13	13	13	13	13	14	14	14	14	14	14
Seasonal stock	25	0	25	0	25	0	25	0	25	0	25	0
Emergency reserves: volume	6	3	8	9	5	9	9	7	17	7	13	8
in days of previous year's demand	11	5	12	14	8	14	14	11	24	10	17	10

[1]These figures are assumed to be 10 percent of the average total stock levels, using the National Petroleum Council's analysis of March 1973 and September 1973 stocks.

TABLE A-13 (continued)

Estimated Emergency Distillate Reserves in the Four Nonexporting Countries

(in millions of barrels)

	1973 High	1973 Low	1974 High	1974 Low	1975 High	1975 Low	1976 High	1976 Low	1977 High	1977 Low	1978 High	1978 Low
GERMANY												
Stock level	62	41	77	55	64	49	64	46	67	54	65	46
Commercial inventories	26	26	22	22	23	23	25	25	25	25	26	26
Seasonal stock	19	0	19	0	19	0	19	0	19	0	19	0
Emergency reserves: volume in days of previous	17	15	36	33	22	26	20	21	23	29	20	20
year's demand	14	12	26	24	21	25	18	18	19	23	16	16
FRANCE												
Stock level	n.a.	n.a.	112	76	95	78	98	58	99	6	84	48
Commercial inventories	n.a.	n.a.	15	15	15	15	15	15	15	1	17	17
Seasonal stock	n.a.	n.a.	36	0	36	0	36	0	36	–	36	0
Emergency reserves: volume in days of previous	n.a.	n.a.	61	61	44	63	47	43	48	4	31	31
year's demand	n.a.	n.a.	69	68	57	81	64	59	61	5	40	40

TABLE A-14

The Trade Factor:
Estimated Emergency Distillate
Reserves in Italy and in the Netherlands

(in millions of barrels)

	1973 High	1973 Low	1974 High	1974 Low	1975 High	1975 Low	1976 High	1976 Low	1977 High	1977 Low	1978 High	1978 Low
1. ITALY												
Stock level	34	16	49	29	31	33	31	19	42	30	34	28
Seasonal stock	9	0	9	0	9	0	9	0	9	0	9	0
Commercial inventories												
a) domestic sales only	7	7	8	8	8	8	9	9	9	9	10	10
b) including regular exports	10	10	10	10	10	10	10	10	12	12	12	12
Emergency reserves: volumes												
a) without export working stocks	18	9	32	21	14	25	13	10	24	21	15	18
b) with export working stocks	15	6	30	19	12	23	12	9	21	18	13	16
Emergency reserves: days of previous year's inland sales												
a) without export working stocks	50	25	87	57	35	63	32	25	52	46	33	40
b) with export working stocks	42	17	82	52	30	58	30	22	46	40	29	36
2. THE NETHERLANDS												
Stock level	19	9	25	17	20	11	19	14	17	10	16	11
Seasonal stock	8	0	8	0	8	0	8	0	8	0	8	0
Commercial inventories												
a) domestic sales only	3	3	3	3	3	3	3	3	3	3	3	3
b) including regular exports	10	10	8	8	8	8	9	9	7	7	10	10
Emergency reserves: volumes												
a) without export working stocks	8	6	14	14	9	8	8	11	6	7	5	8
b) with export working stocks	1	0	9	9	4	3	2	5	2	3	0	1
Emergency reserves: days of previous year's inland sales												
a) without export working stocks	49	40	97	97	73	66	65	85	41	47	35	57
b) with export working stocks	7	0	59	59	32	25	20	41	14	30	0	7

APPENDIX

TABLE A-15

Average Residual Oil Stocks

(in millions of barrels)

	1973	1974	1975	1976	1977	1978
U.S.A.	51	55	72	70	79	76
Japan	39	44	39	42	43	44
Germany	22	21	21	18	19	17.9
France	--	34	38	31	29	32.8
Italy	36	34	35	27	39	38.3
The Netherlands	13	14	13	11	13	12.0

TABLE A-16

Average Residual Oil Stocks

(in days of inland sales)

	1973	1974	1975	1976	1977	1978
U.S.A.	18	21	29	25	25	28
Japan	17	20	20	21	21	21
Germany	40	47	52	41	46	43
France	n.a.	55	75	52	55	61
Italy	49	45	51	40	54	53
The Netherlands	144	233	260	183	288	155

TABLE A-17

Estimated Emergency Reserves of
Residual Oil in the Four Nonexporting Countries

(in millions of barrels)

	1973 High	Low	1974 High	Low	1975 High	Low	1976 High	Low	1977 High	Low	1978 High	Low
1. U.S.A.[1]												
Stock level	55	43	61	45	83	64	79	64	96	65	90	62
Seasonal stock	16	0	16	0	16	0	16	0	16	0	16	0
Commercial inventories	28	28	26	26	25	25	23	23	31	31	27	27
Emergency reserves: volume	11	15	19	19	42	39	40	41	49	34	47	35
in days of previous year's domestic demand	4	6	7	7	16	15	16	16	18	12	17	13
2. JAPAN												
Stock level	43	35	50	40	45	34	46	35	48	34	49	41
Seasonal stock	10	0	10	0	10	0	10	0	10	0	10	0
Commercial inventories	25	25	25	25	23	23	22	22	20	20	21	21
Emergency reserves: volume	8	10	15	15	12	11	14	13	18	14	18	20
in days of previous year's domestic demand	4	5	7	7	6	5	7	7	8	7	9	10

[1]The National Petroleum Council report indicates that only 0.5 percent of U.S.
residual oil stocks are in pipeline

APPENDIX

TABLE A-17 (continued)

Estimated Emergency Reserves of
Residual Oil in the Four Nonexporting Countries

(in millions of barrels)

	1973 High	Low	1974 High	Low	1975 High	Low	1976 High	Low	1977 High	Low	1978 High	Low
3. GERMANY												
Stock level	26	18	26	18	23	16	20	16	21	17	20	16
Seasonal stock	7	0	7	0	7	0	7	0	7	0	7	0
Commercial inventories	6	6	5	5	4	4	4	4	4	4	4	4
Emergency reserves: volume	13	12	14	13	12	12	9	12	10	13	9	12
in days of previous year's domestic sales	24	22	26	24	27	27	22	30	22	29	22	29
4. FRANCE												
Stock level	n.a.	n.a.	42	28	42	34	36	26	33	26	35	26
Seasonal stock	n.a.	n.a.	9	0	9	0	9	0	9	0	9	0
Commercial inventories	n.a.	n.a.	7	7	6	6	7	7	5	5	5	5
Emergency reserves: volume	n.a.	n.a.	26	21	27	28	20	19	19	21	21	21
in days of previous year's domestic sales	n.a.	n.a.	42	34	43	44	38	36	30	34	40	40

TABLE A-18

The Trade Factor: Estimated Emergency Reserves
of Residual Fuel Oil in Italy and in the Netherlands

(in millions of barrels)

| | 1973 | | 1974 | | 1975 | | 1976 | | 1977 | | 1978 | |
	High	Low	High	Low	High	Low	High	Low	High	Low	High	Low
1. ITALY												
Stock level	44	29	39	29	42	28	31	23	45	33	42	35
Season stock	12	0	12	0	12	0	12	0	12	0	12	0
Commercial inventories												
a) domestic sales and bunkers	8	8	9	9	8	8	8	8	8	8	8	8
b) including regular exports	10	10	10	10	9	9	8	8	9	9	9	9
Emergency reserves: volumes												
a) without export working stocks	24	21	18	20	22	20	11	15	25	25	22	27
b) with export working stocks	22	19	17	19	21	19	11	15	24	24	21	26
Emergency reserves: days of previous year's domestic sales												
a) without export working stocks	33	29	25	27	29	27	16	22	37	37	30	37
b) with export working stocks	30	26	23	26	28	26	16	22	36	36	29	35
2. NETHERLANDS												
Stock level	14	12	16	11	16	11	12	10	16	11	14	10
Seasonal stock	4	0	4	0	4	0	4	0	4	0	4	0
Commercial inventories												
a) domestic sales and bunkers	3	3	2	2	2	2	2	2	2	2	2	2
b) including regular exports	5	5	4	4	4	4	4	4	4	4	4	4
Emergency reserves: volumes												
a) without export working stocks	7	9	10	9	10	9	6	8	10	9	8	8
b) with export working stocks	5	7	8	7	8	7	4	6	8	7	6	6
Emergency reserves: days of previous year's domestic sales												
a) without export working stocks	67	86	116	105	159	143	125	167	222	200	181	181
b) with export working stock	48	67	93	81	126	111	83	125	178	156	136	136

APPENDIX

TABLE A-19

Summary of Estimated Emergency
Reserves in Product Stocks

(in millions of barrels)

		1973	1974	1975	1976	1977	1978
1.	U.S.A.						
	Gasoline	41	52	56	51	70	45
	Distillate	35	49	70	61	71	54
	Residual	13	19	41	41	42	41
2.	JAPAN						
	Gasoline	3	4	3	4	3	2
	Distillate	5	9	7	8	12	10
	Residual	9	15	12	14	16	19
3.	GERMANY						
	Gasoline	10	9	9	8	9	7
	Distillate	16	35	24	21	26	20
	Residual	13	14	12	11	12	11
4	FRANCE						
	Gasoline	n.a.	19	16	15	18	17
	Distillate	n.a.	61	53	45	47	31
	Residual	n.a.	24	28	20	20	21
5.	ITALY						
	Gasoline	5	7	5	6	13	11
	Distillate	14	27	20	12	23	17
	Residual	23	19	21	13	25	25
6.	THE NETHERLANDS						
	Gasoline	4	4	4	4	4	3
	Distillate	7	14	9	10	7	7
	Residual	8	10	10	7	10	8

NOTES: 1. When seasonal fluctuations necessitated "high" and "low" estimates, an average of the two has been used for this table.

2. The Italian and Dutch figures exclude export working stocks.

TABLE A-20

Estimated Emergency Reserves of

Crude Oil and Principal Petroleum Products

(in days of previous year's net imports)

	1973	1974	1975	1976	1977	1978
U.S.A.[1]	32	31	40	38	37	33
Japan[1]	21	29	31	35	38	45
Germany[1]	21	28	31	40	45	46
France	n.a.	62	61	55	59	48
Italy	37	46	42	37	45	41
Netherlands	56	85	93	101	85	81

[1] Including government strategic reserves

TABLE A-21

Net Oil Imports of Selected Countries, 1972-77
(in thousands of barrels per day)

Year	U.S.A.	Japan	Germany	France	Italy	Netherlands
1972	4,273	4,136	2,599	2,191	1,776	541
1973	5,776	4,835	2,824	2,466	1,929	564
1974	5,604	4,871	2,580	2,427	1,976	525
1975	5,582	4,426	2,397	1,986	1,711	417
1976	7,059	4,789	2,665	2,123	1,848	526
1977	8,376	4,995	2,609	2,128	1,819	419

Source: Organization for Economic Cooperation and Development,
Quarterly Oil Statistics (Paris: O.E.C.D.).

Notes

•

CHAPTER 1

1. Figures from the *Petroleum Economist* 46 (April 1979): 177.

2. Edward R. Fried and Charles L. Schultz, eds., *Higher Oil Prices and the World Economy* (Washington, D.C.: The Brookings Institution, 1975), p. 18.

3. These terms are defined in chapter 7.

4. There is a third broad option: requiring consumers to hold emergency stocks. In spite of the obvious logistical advantages of each consumer's holding his own emergency supplies, this option is rarely practical politically (for the obvious reason that consumers, like oil companies, would dislike such an obligation, and unlike oil companies, could penalize a government by voting it out of office) or economically (it costs much more to store oil in small batches than in large batches).

5. See appendix.

6. *Implicitly* because the IEP treats all member countries the same way, regardless of the quality of their emergency reserves. See chapter 4.

7. The difficulty arises not only because it is hard to quantify the effect of oil losses but also because toleration itself is so much a function of subjective factors. A society would be willing to suffer more for a popular cause than for an unpopular one.

8. The focus here is on defensive measures. Obviously, governments can also take offensive measures. One could say that among the reasons for having emergency reserves, one would be to prevent, or at least delay, recourse to offensive measures.

9. For most oil-importing countries, these measures do not provide much relief. Countries with indigenous oil resources probably are producing as much as they can, and using all the domestic coal and gas available, simply because oil imports are so expensive today.

10. Including the advertising of "phantom measures" as real ones—e.g., oil stocks that really are not emergency reserves. See chapter 7.

11. These are arbitrary numbers. See chapter 8.

12. Presumably, the government would not want to deplete the emergency stock, but where would it decide to stop? Almost any "floor" on drawdowns (i.e., a level of emergency reserves that "cannot" be used because it must be retained for contingencies) will seem like the bottom of the tank. This built-in resistance to stock drawdowns is discussed further in chapter 8.

155

CHAPTER 2

1. Irvine H. Anderson, Jr., *The Standard-Vacuum Oil Company and United States East Asian Policy, 1933-1941* (Princeton: Princeton University Press, 1975), pp. 191-92.

2. Ibid., pp. 227-28.

3. Organization for Economic Cooperation and Development, *Quarterly Oil Statistics, Third Quarter 1978* (Paris: OECD, 1978), p. 294.

4. "Economic Interdependence and National Security," in *Economic Issues and National Security*, ed. Klaus Knorr and Frank M. Trager (Lawrence, Kans.: National Security Education Program, 1977), p. 8.

5. Ibid.

6. See chapter 3 for more details.

7. See chapter 3 and Robert S. Stobaugh, "The Oil Companies in Crisis," in *The Oil Crisis in Perspective*, ed. Raymond Vernon, *Daedalus* (Journal of the Academy of Arts and Sciences) 104 (Fall 1975): 179-202.

8. "The Oil Price Outlook's Bad—And a Saudi Decision Did It," *The Economist*, May 26, 1979, pp. 101-5.

9. This recommendation was discussed at the summit meeting or the major industrial countries in June 1979. Agreement was reached to establish a monthly register of all crude imports. Registration began in November 1979. A register of product imports will be established in 1980. *Platt's Oilgram News* (New York: McGraw-Hill), September 27, 1979, and October 12, 1979.

10. For a valuable survey of 78 forecasts issued since 1973, see the International Energy Agency, *A Comparison of Energy Projections to 1984*, IEA Monograph no. 1 (Paris: Organization for Economic Cooperation and Development, January 1979).

11. U.S. Central Intelligence Agency, *The International Energy Situation: Outlook to 1985* (Washington, D.C.: Government Printing Office, April 1977), p. 18.

12. Ibid.

13. See *Working Paper on International Energy Supply: A Perspective from the Industrial World* (New York: The Rockefeller Foundation, May 1978).

14. Walter Levy, "Oil Policy and OPEC Development," *Foreign Affairs* 57 (Winter 1978/79): 298-99.

15. Ibid.

16. This section is a revised version of the author's *Oil and Security: Problems and Prospects of Importing Countries*, Adelphi Paper no. 136 (London: International Institute for Strategic Studies, 1977), pp. 3-7.

17. *International Herald Tribune*, November 22, 1973.

18. Address to *Time* magazine luncheon, January 17, 1975; declassified State Department transcript.

19. U.S. oil production is declining: in 1973 it was 10.9 million b/d; in 1974, 10.5 million b/d; in 1975, 10.0 million b/d. In 1978, the increase in Alaskan production boosted U.S. output to 10.3 million b/d. Figures are taken from U.S., Department of Energy, Energy Information Administration, Office of Energy Data and Interpretation, *Energy Data Reports*, December 1973, 1974, 1975, and 1978, p. 2 (table 1).

20. David R. McDonald, U.S. Department of the Treasury Memorandum, "Report of Investigation of the Effects of Petroleum Imports and Petroleum Products on the National Security Pursuant to Sec. 232 of the Trade Expansion Act, As Amended," January 13, 1975.

21. Ibid.

22. U.S. Federal Energy Administration, *Project Independence Report* (Washington, D.C.: Government Printing Office, November 1974). pp. 364-69.

23. Richard N. Cooper, *National Resources and National Security in the Middle East*

and the International System, Part II: Security and the Energy Crisis, Adelphi Paper no. 115 (London: International Institute for Strategic Studies, 1974), p. 8, cited in the author's *Oil and Security.*

24. See, for instance, Mansfield, *A Short History of OPA* (Office of Temporary Controls, Office of Price Administration, 1948), as cited in National Petroleum Council, *Emergency Preparation for Interruption of Petroleum Imports into the United States,* Supplemental Papers to Interim Report of November 15, 1973 (Washington, D.C.: NPC, December 21, 1973), p. 87.

23. Wolfgang Hager, *Europe's Economic Security* (Paris: Atlantic Institute, February 1976), pp. 15-16.

26. See "The Oil Price Outlook's Bad."

27. The 1965 and 1969 estimates are from the Cabinet Task Force on Oil Import Control, *The Oil Import Question: A Report on the Relationship of Oil Imports to the National Security* (Washington, D.C.: Government Printing Office, 1971), pp. 213-46.

28. As will be discussed in chapter 8, oil stocks play a critical role in this process.

29. Such diversions can be a complex undertaking. See chapters 3-5.

CHAPTER 3

1. For a useful summary of developments, see U.S. Congress, Senate, Committee on Foreign Relations, *U.S. Oil Companies and the Arab Oil Embargo* (Washington, D.C.: Government Printing Office, January 1975).

2. Exxon, Mobil, Texaco, Standard Oil of California, Gulf, Royal Dutch/Shell, and British Petroleum. Among other important companies are Ente Nazionale Idrocarburi (ENI) of Italy and Compagnie Française des Pètroles (CFP) of France.

3. U.S. Senate, Committee on Foreign Relations, *U.S. Oil Companies,* p. 7.

4. U.S. Congress, Senate, Committee on Foreign Relations, Subcommittee on Multinational Corporations, *Hearings: Multinational Corporations and U.S. Foreign Policy, Part 9* (Washington, D.C.: Government Printing Office, 1975), p. 142.

5. Ibid.

6. Some evaluations of the embargo do not take product trade into account at all. For example, see Robert B. Stobaugh, "The Oil Companies in the Crisis," in *The Oil Crisis in Perspective,* ed. Raymond Vernon, *Daedalus* (Journal of the Academy of Arts and Sciences) 104 (Fall 1975): 179-202. This issue of *Daedalus* contains numerous articles evaluating the political and economic implications of the oil crisis.

7. See tables in Organization for Economic Cooperation and Development, *Oil Statistics* (Paris: OECD, 1975).

8. This action resulted in various levels of oil prices, which led the government to establish a still-controversial program "equalizing" the price of crude oil to all U.S. refineries.

9. Commission of the European Communities, *Report by the Commission on the Behavior of the Oil Companies in the Community During the Period from October 1973 to March 1974* (Brussels: European Economic Community, December 1976), p. 102.

10. Ibid., p. 92.

11. Ibid., p. 101. See also International Research Group, *Energy: The Recent Crisis and Future Prospects of the European Community and Japan,* report prepared for the U.S. Federal Energy Administration under contract no. 14-01-0001-2027 (Washington, D.C.: IRG, August 1974).

12. This conclusion cannot be applied to France, because monthly product-stock data for 1973 and 1974 are not comparable. See the Appendix.

13. *Strategic Survey, 1973* (London: International Institute for Strategic Studies, 1974), p. 62.

14. *Platt's Oilgram Price Service* (New York: McGraw-Hill), January 11, 1974.

15. For a discussion of these postcrisis bilateral deals, see International Research Group, *Energy: The Resent Crisis,* pp. 45-57. For a comparative evaluation of French and German responses to the oil crisis, see Horst Mendershausen, *Coping with the Oil Crisis* (Baltimore: The Johns Hopkins University Press, 1976).

16. Commission of the European Communities, *Report . . . on the Behaviour of the Oil Companies,* p. 65.

17. For an evaluation of the U.S. oil allocation program, see Mason Willrich, *Administration of Energy Shortages: Natural Gas and Petroleum* (Cambridge, Mass.: Ballinger Publishing Co., 1976), pp. 179-204; and *Report of the Presidential Task Force on Reform of Federal Energy Administration Regulations,* prepared for the Council of Economic Advisors, 2 vols. (Washington, D.C.: National Technical Information Service, December 1976).

18. Commission of the European Communities, *Report . . . on the Behaviour of the Oil Companies,* pp. 77-78.

19. *Platt's Oilgram News Service* (New York: McGraw-Hill), January 10, 1974.

20. U.S. Federal Energy Administration, *Project Independence Report* (Washington, D.C.: Government Printing Office, November 1974), p. 288.

CHAPTER 4

1. The OECD members are the United States, Canada, Belgium, Denmark, France, the Federal Republic of Germany, Ireland, Italy, Luxembourg, the Netherlands, the United Kingdom, Austria, Finland, Greece, Iceland, Norway, Portugal, Spain, Sweden, Switzerland, Turkey, New Zealand, Australia, and Japan.

2. Organization of Arab Petroleum Exporting Countries, whose members are Algeria, Bahrain, Egypt, Iraq, Kuwait, Libya, Saudi Arabia, Syria, and the United Arab Emirates.

3. Mason Willrich and Melvin A. Conant, "The International Energy Agency: An Interpretation and Assessment," *American Journal of Comparative Law* 71 (April 1977): 211.

4. See U.S. Federal Energy Administration, *Project Independence Report* (Washington, D.C.: Government Printing Office, November 1974).

5. The sixteenth original signatories of the agreement are the United States, Canada, the Federal Republic of Germany, Italy, the Netherlands, Belgium, Luxembourg, Denmark, Ireland, the United Kingdom, Austria, Spain, Sweden, Switzerland, Turkey, and Japan. Australia, New Zealand, and Greece joined later, and Norway is an associate member. The text of the agreement can be found in U.S. Congress, Senate, Committee on Interior and Insular Affairs, *Agreement on an International Energy Program* (Washington, D.C.: Government Printing Office, 1974): hereafter referred to as the *IEP Agreement.*

6. Willrich and Conant, "International Energy Agency," p. 201.

7. Statement by the Acting Assistant Secretary of State for Economic and Business Affairs, *IEP Agreement,* pp. 21-22.

8. Willrich and Conant, "International Energy Agency," p. 210.

9. It is highly unlikely that a participating country might have "used up a substantial part of its emergency reserves" as a result of this delay, a concern voiced by Willrich and Conant, ibid.

10. Ibid., p. 211.

11. See chapter 8.

12. This represents average consumption during the previous four quarters for which statistics are available (i.e., there is a one-quarter lag in the availability of the data).

13. According to the agreement, stock drawdown is determined by a member's share of the group emergency reserve commitment; but since this commitment is based on net imports, the drawdown obligation is a function of each member's import share.

14. It is "so-called" because a country can consume what it wants. The IEA numbers are guidelines as far as domestic programs are concerned.

15. In fact, however, Britain will continue to import about 50 percent of the oil it requires and export about 50 percent of the oil it produces because its North Sea oil can attract a premium on the world market due to its low-sulphur content and high specific gravity. These qualities make it easier to produce cleaner-burning, "light" finished products such as gasoline.

CHAPTER 5

1. The following discussion is based on the test-run briefings the author received from the IEA and various national governments.

2. Companies still will be torn between their duty to their stockholders—i.e., to make good profits—and their commitment to the IEP sharing scheme. A crisis is likely to produce countless such trade-offs, and each company is likely to develop its own approach to this "game-theoretic" optimization situation.

3. This is in the first month of the crisis. In the second month, the IEA will fold in any imbalances remaining from the first month. In subsequent months, it will carry over imbalances from the previous two months to forecast allocation rights and obligations for the next three months.

4. Some governments, of course, will be more willing buyers than others.

5. A company feeling wronged by such an order can appeal to whatever higher national authority can countermand such orders.

6. In accordance with section 252 of the Energy Policy and Conservation Act (EPCA) (42 U.S.C. 6201), the U.S. Federal Trade Commission, the principal antitrust authority, and the Department of Justice must monitor the activities of U.S. oil companies involved in the IEP, including their participation in the test runs. For the purpose of the test runs, the FTC held that "oil company participants [are] not permitted . . . to exchange current, commercially sensitive information." See U.S. Federal Trade Commission, *Second Report to the Congress and the President Pursuant to the Energy Policy and Conservation Act of 1975* (Washington, D.C.: FTC, March 21, 1977).

7. See chapter 3.

CHAPTER 6

1. A system of production controls.

2. *Report of the Presidential Task Force on Reform of Federal Energy Administration Regulations,* prepared for the Council of Economic Advisors, 2 vols. (Washington, D.C.: National Technical Information Service, December 1976), 2: D-66 and D-67.

3. Ibid., 1: 20.

4. A recent example of this attitude is the Senate's approval of a "sunset bill" providing for the automatic expiration of government spending programs every ten years if they are not reauthorized. See the *Washington Post*, October 12, 1978.

5. For a discussion of the Energy Policy and Conservation Act's guidance concerning the size of the Strategic Petroleum Reserve, see chapter 7.

6. Submitted to Congress in December 1976. See Federal Energy Administration,

Strategic Petroleum Reserve Plan (Washington, D.C.: Government Printing Office, December 15, 1976).

7. *Strategic Petroleum Reserve Plan: Amendment No. 1, Acceleration of the Development Schedule, Energy Action No. 12* (Washington, D.C.: Federal Energy Administration, Strategic Petroleum Reserve Office, March 1977), and *Strategic Petroleum Reserve Plan: Amendment No. 2, Expansion of the Strategic Petroleum Reserve, Energy Action DOE No. 1* (Washington, D.C.: Department of Energy, Strategic Petroleum Reserve Office, March 1978).

8. Projections to 1982 are from *Strategic Petroleum Reserve Plan: Amendment No. 2;* projections to 1985 were provided in conversations with Department of Energy officials.

9. Section 156(a) of the Act and chapter 7 of this volume.

10. The DOE maintained that industry would not enjoy a cost advantage over the government in building emergency reserves and that, therefore, the overall cost of an industrial petroleum reserve to consumers would be greater. Federal Energy Administration, *Plan,* p. 146.

11. In the summer of 1978, the U.S. Office of Management and Budget encouraged the DOE to study ways in which the funds for the last 250 or 500 million barrels could be acquired elsewhere than from the federal budget. The DOE commissioned studies (some of which the author was involved in) of alternative funding options, including special import levies and the establishment of an industrial petroleum reserve. These were submitted to the Secretary of Energy for consideration and again were rejected in favor of a federal Strategic Petroleum Reserve.

12. Depending upon whether a refiner obtains his crude from domestic, "old" (price-controlled) oil or from foreign sources, he is either required to sell or entitled to purchase "entitlements," which have the effect of standardizing the price of U.S. crude oil. In 1977, the average national composite price for crude oil was $11.96 per barrel, compared with an average import price for crude of $14.53. See U.S. Department of Energy, Energy Information Administration, *Monthly Energy Review* (Washington, D.C.: National Technical Information Service, July 1978).

13. See Federal Energy Administration, *Plan,* p. 17. This estimate assumes that the SPR will be obtained at the average national composite price and that there will be no increase in world oil prices to 1980.

14. Ibid., pp. 188-90.

15. U.S. Department of Energy, Strategic Petroleum Reserve Office, *The 1978 Annual Report* (Washington, D.C.: DOE, March 1979).

16. Thomas J. Moore, "Saudis Vetoed Filling of Oil Reserve," *Chicago Sun-Times,* April 10, 1980, p. 5.

17. See U.S. Department of Energy, *The Role of Foreign Governments in the Energy Industries* (Washington, D.C.: Government Printing Office, October 1977), p. 323.

18. Ibid., p. 322.

19. *Japan Petroleum Weekly* (Tokyo: Japan Petroleum Consultants, Ltd.), August 9, 1976.

20. For a definition of the IEA requirements, see chapter 7.

21. Law No. 96 of 1975, December 17, 1975. An English copy of the law was obtained from MITI.

22. MITI Ordinance No. 26 of 1975, art. 9.

23. Estimates provided by the Institute for Energy Economics, Tokyo, but attributed to MITI.

24. MITI, "Petroleum Policy Measures," June 1977. A copy of this memorandum was obtained from a Japanese oil company.

25. At the same time, the corporation's name was changed to the Japan National Oil Corporation.

26. A kiloliter equals about 6.3 barrels.

27. This information was provided through correspondence with the Institute of Energy Economics, Tokyo. According to U.S. government sources, in October 1978 JNOC's stockpile target was raised to 30 million kiloliters by 1985.

28. The estimates are from the Institute of Energy Economics, the Japan Petroleum Association, and Mitsubishi Oil Company.

29. *The Economist,* October 1, 1977, notes the example of Niijima Island, where residents are fiercely resisting government/industry efforts to construct a tank farm that could meet up to one-third of Japan's incremental storage needs.

30. U.S. Congress, Senate, Committee on Interior and Insular Affairs, *A Study of the Relationships Between the Government and the Petroleum Industry in Selected Foreign Countries: The Federal Republic of Germany,* prepared by the Congressional Research Service (Washington, D.C.: Government Printing Office, 1975), pp. 3–4.

31. U.S. Department of Energy, *The Role of Foreign Governments in the Energy Industries,* p. 128.

32. The 1975 law is the "Gesetz über Mindestvorraten an Erdölzeugnissen," printed in the *Bundesgesetzblatt,* September 16, 1975.

33. *Platt's Oilgram News Service* (New York: McGraw-Hill), June 24, 1976.

34. Ibid., July 2, 1976.

35. "Memorandum on the Foundation of a Corporation Under Public Law for the Purpose of Compulsory Storage of Petroleum Products," Mineralölwirtschaftsverband E.V. and Aussenhandelsverband E.V., January 1977, p. 1. Copy obtained from a German oil company.

36. Ibid.

37. The maximum amount of this transaction is estimated to be 17 million tons, or about 124 million barrels.

38. On July 25, 1978, the Bundestag passed a law paving the way for the establishment of the EBV. Article 18 of this law provides for the establishment of a tax or fee (*Beitrag*) to be collected by the oil industry for payment to the EBV. See Bundesgesetzblatt, Teil I, "Gesetz Über die Bevorratung mit Erdöl und Erdölzeugnissen," 41 (Bonn, July 29, 1978), pp. 1073–84.

39. This amounts to a "tax" of about 0.6 pfennig per liter (about 0.3 U.S. cents per gallon).

40. The EBV will own or lease oil storage facilities all over Germany because it will acquire the facilities refiners and importers have had to build to comply with the storage obligations. These facilities will be dispersed, not centrally located.

41. The EBV probably will acquire some stocks of finished products that must be "turned over" periodically. However, the timing of these turnovers must be negotiated between the EBV and the oil companies.

42. The International Energy Agency and the European Economic Community.

43. "Gesetz über Mindestvorraten," art. 15.

44. "Memorandum on the Foundation of a Corporation," p. 8.

45. From article 1 of the law. The law and subsequent decrees can be found in *Réglementation Pétrolière: Part A, Régime de l'importation des produits pétrolières* (Paris: Comité Professionnel du Pétrole, 1976).

46. Storage decrees can be found in ibid., *Part F,* Réglementation des stocks de réserve.

47. Ibid.

48. In the early 1970s, the French government considered but rejected building a

supplementary government reserve, according to the *Europe Oil Telegram* (Hamburg, Germany), July 22, 1974.

49. It was a fortunate coincidence that Italy—at the time the only other EEC member with long-standing storage regulations—also imposed the obligation on the private sector.

50. EEC estimates are taken from Commission of the European Communities, *Report by the Commission on the Behaviour of the Oil Companies in the Community During the Period from October 1973 to March 1974* (Brussels: European Economic Community, December 1976), p. 143.

51. However, a number of French refineries were amalgamated into Elf in the 1960s.

52. The French oil market has been referred to as the "gilded cage."

53. This information was provided by the French government.

54. U.S. Congress, Senate, Committee on Interior and Insular Affairs, *A study of the Relationships Between Governments and the Petroleum Industry in Selected Foreign Countries: Italy,* prepared by the Congressional Research Service (Washington, D.C.: Government Printing Office, 1975).

55. ENI's numerous subsidiaries are involved in the production and handling of all the energy fuels as well as in engineering, construction, and even in hotel and newspaper enterprises. For an interesting account of ENI's development, see Paul Frankel, *Mattei: Oil and Power Politics* (London: Faber and Faber, 1966).

56. U.S. Senate, Committee on Interior and Insular Affairs, *Italy,* p. 6.

57. *Petroleum Economist,* November 1975.

58. U.S. Senate, Committee on Interior and Insular Affaris, *Italy,* p. 6.

59. "R.D.L. November 2, 1973, No. 1741: Disciplina dell'importazione, della lavorazione, del deposito e della destribuzione degli oli minerali e dei carburanti," *Gazetta Ufficiale,* no. 301, December 30, 1933.

60. "R.D. July 20, 1934, No. 1303: Approvazione del regolamento per l'esecuzione del R.D.L. 2/11/33, No. 1741 . . . ," *Gazetta Ufficiale,* no. 191, August 16, 1934; amended by the Ministerial Decree of August 13, 1968, "Variazzione della misura della scorta di reserva a carica dei concessionari dei depositi di prodotti petrolifieri derivati," *Gazetta Ufficiale,* no. 232, September 12, 1968. A 70-day storage requirement was levied by the Ministry of Industry and Commerce in its "Circolare no. 427" of July 14, 1961, and was raised to 90 days by the Ministry's Letter no. 92 of August 20, 1976. The Ministry does not need legislative approval to change refineries' storage requirements, but does need it to change those of non-oil industry storage tank owners.

61. This applies only to storage capacity exceeding 200 cubic meters. (A cubic meter of storage capacity holds about six barrels of oil.)

62. This includes only owners of storage capacity exceeding 3,000 cubic meters. Owners of 200-3,000 cubic meters of storage capacity are obliged to comply with the 20 percent provision, but their oil is not included in the government's calculation of the national storage target.

63. See the appendix for a discussion of the Italian oil industry's stockpile levels.

64. For further discussion of the influence of exports on emergency reserve estimates, see the Appendix.

65. This was the only such informal and trusting arrangement encountered in this survey. The term *gentlemen's agreement* is not the author's shorthand, but the term used by Dutch officials and found in EEC storage memoranda describing the old Dutch program.

66. Ministerie van Economische Zaken, *Interim Centraal Organ Voorraadvorming Aardolieprodukten* (Final report of the Project Group on the ICO), July 31, 1978, p. 2. Provided by the Ministry of Economic Affairs, The Hague, the Netherlands.

67. "De Wet van 21 Oktober 1976," *Staatsblad van het Koninkrijk der Nederlanden,* January 1976, sec. 569.

68. These still-tentative program details were listed in a memorandum dated September 19, 1977, sent to the Dutch Parliament by the Minister of Economics and given to the author by ministry officials.

69. The interim CSO was scheduled to come into existence in early 1979. The Iranian crisis, however, forced a delay in plans. It now appears that the interim CSO will go into business in 1980.

70. Ministerie van Economische Zaken, *Interim Centraal Orgaan,* pp. I-1 and I-2.

71. Ibid.

CHAPTER 7

1. For a more extended discussion of this point, see pages 85-86.

2. This is the International Energy Agency's standard for measuring stockpiles. See pages 87-88.

3. This is said with full knowledge of the government's periodic statements to the contrary to the IEA. The State Department has represented commercial stocks to the IEA as emergency reserves, whereby the U.S. has met its IEP obligation. For a critique of this inconsistency, see Comptroller General of the United States, *Report to the Congress: Issues Needing Attention in Developing the Strategic Petroleum Reserve* (Washington, D.C.: General Accounting Office, February 16, 1977). IEP stockpile definitions allow this to occur, but the U.S. Department of Energy does not treat commercial inventories as emergency reserves in its crisis planning. At most, oil company stocks will "bridge" the time lag required to deploy the SPR. A study conducted for the U.S. Department of State concluded that U.S. "excess stocks," defined as those that could be drawn down without causing major supply constraints, "might permit the substitution of 21 days of total oil imports" at the 1974 import rate of 6.1 million b/d. See John Lichtblau, "Petroleum Inventories in the United States—Current Levels and Availabilities," mimeograped (New York: Petroleum Industry Research Foundation, Inc., September 19, 1974), pp. 11 and 13.

4. Some Department of Energy officials claim they are not. Their argument stems from the point that the oil industry has *no* incentive to maintain excess stocks under normal business circumstances. The rebuttal, of course, is that when circumstances become abnormal, steps can be taken to streamline the system to "liberate" some of the commercial safety stocks.

5. The meeting was attended by government officials from the United Kingdom, the United States, Germany, France, and the Netherlands; by officials from the International Energy Agency and the Commission of the European Economic Community; and by oil industry officials from the United Kingdom, the United States, Italy, and France.

6. The paper discussed at the meeting was prepared by this author. The same methodology used in the appendix to estimate emergency reserve levels was used in the discussion paper.

7. The U.S. Federal Energy Administration expressed a very pessimistic view of the "real reserves" in other IEA countries. It estimated that current "real estimates of actual usable reserves are only 20 days. Most countries would not be able to identify those quantities of stocks that could actually be used during an emergency." From an FEA memorandum to Senator Henry Jackson dated March 16, 1977, and reprinted in U.S. Congress, Senate, Committee on Interior and Insular Affairs, *Hearings: Review of the*

Strategic Petroleum Reserve Plan (Washington, D.C.: Government Printing Office, 1977), Publication no. 95-10, p. 408.

8. Energy Policy and Conservation Act, 42 U.S.C. 6201, sec. 156 (a).

9. Ibid., sec. 156 (B).

10. The argument rested essentially on the proposition that only the government could achieve significant economies of scale. The department did not mention the German-Dutch notion of establishing a third party that would store the collective obligations of the companies. See U.S. Federal Energy Administration, *Strategic Petroleum Reserve Plan* (Washington, D.C.: Government Printing Office, December 15, 1976), p. 146.

11. About 180 importers and 150 refining companies potentially would have to comply with an IPR obligation, according to a contract study prepared for the DOE. See JRB Associates, Inc., *Feasibility Study for Requiring Storage of Crude Oil, Residual Fuel Oil, and/or Refined Petroleum Products by Industry* (Vienna, Va.: January 15, 1977), Contract no. CO-05-60477-00 (as amended).

12. Federal Energy Administration, *Plan,* p. 141.

13. The author was involved in these discussions as a contractor to the DOE, producing a report analyzing the implications of foreign "IPR" programs under the title *Industrial Petroleum Reserve Programs in Six Foreign Nations* (Washington, D.C., September 7, 1978), Contract no. EL-78-X-01-4848, and as a consultant to a firm that provided much of the DOE's staff work for this investigation.

14. Shared pipelines and large storage terminals lead to large cargo sizes for individual company shipments, and hence to larger cycle stocks. The same process occurs with tanker deliveries: shipments from very large crude-oil carriers require importers to keep larger cycle stocks on hand than do shipments from smaller tankers.

15. Council Directive 68/414/EEC, December 20, 1968, art. 1, in Commission of the European Communities, *Community Energy Policy* (Brussels: ECC, 1976), p. 192.

16. International Energy Agreement, art. 2, reprinted in U.S. Congress, Senate, Committee on Interior and Insular Affairs, *Hearings: International Energy Program* (Washington, D.C.: Government Printing Office, 1975), p. 000; hereafter cited as *Hearings: IEP.*

17. Ibid., p. 34.

18. IEP Agreement, Annex, art. 1, reprinted in U.S. Congress, Senate, Committee on Interior and Insular Affairs, *Hearings: IEP,* p. 22.

19. Ibid.; semicolons added.

20. Fuel for international shipping.

21. IEP Agreement, Annex, art. 1, reprinted in U.S. Senate, Committee on Interior and Insular Affairs, *Hearings: IEP,* p. 22; semicolons added.

22. Ibid.

23. Ibid., p. 34.

24. Ibid., p. 33.

25. U.S. Congress, Senate, Committee on Interior and Insular Affairs, *Hearings: Review of the Strategic Petroleum Reserve Plan* (Washington, D.C.: Government Printing Office, 1977), p. 408.

26. National Petroleum Council, *Petroleum Storage for National Security* (Washington, D.C.: NPC, August 1975); and idem, *Emergency Preparedness for Interruption of Petroleum Imports into the United States* (Washington, D.C.: NPC, September, 1974).

27. U.S. Federal Energy Administration, *Project Independence Report* (Washington, D.C.: Government Printing Office, November 1974).

28. Energy Policy and Conservation Act of December 1975 (42 U.S.C. 6201). Section 154 states that the seven-year target should equal the "total volume of crude oil imported into the United States during ... the period of the three consecutive months during the 24-month period preceding the date of enactment of this Act in which average monthly

import levels were the highest." See Federal Energy Administration, *Plan*, p. 24. The three appropriate consecutive months are August, September, and October 1975. The sum of crude-oil imports during these months was 495 million barrels.

29. Federal Energy Administration, *Plan*, p. 10.

30. *Strategic Petroleum Reserve Plan: Amendment No. 2, Expansion of the Strategic Petroleum Reserve, Energy Action DOE No. 1* (Washington, D.C.: Department of Energy, Strategic Petroleum Reserve Office, March 1978), p. 9.

31. Ibid.

32. The National Energy Plan is reprinted in U.S. Congress, Senate, Committee on Energy and Natural Resources, *The President's Energy Program* (Washington, D.C.: Government Printing Office, 1977), Publication no. 95-6.

33. See the *Washington Post*, September 27, 1978, for a summary article of congressional actions of the President's plan.

34. However, the refusal of Congress to approve the COET is not the end of the story. Under the provisions of the legislation that established price controls on crude oil, the President has the power to abolish the controls in the spring of 1979. In May 1979, the President decided to phase out price controls, but given the impact of the sharp price increases experienced in the summer of 1979, Congress may reimpose price control legislation.

35. *Strategic Petroleum Reserve Plan: Amendment No. 2*, p. 11.

36. And to relate it to the emergency reserve levels of other IEA members. See chapter 8.

37. The fact that an antagonist may not want to cause serious damage does not seriously weaken the argument.

38. *Strategic Petroleum Reserve Plan: Amendment No. 2*, p. 14.

39. Ibid. By the end of 1980, however, SPR drawdown capacity was expected to be no more than one million b/d.

40. In Germany and the Netherlands, the EBV and the CSO, respectively, will own or lease the storage tanks in which emergency reserves are kept. However, these storage sites originally belonged to the oil companies and thus are likely to be readily accessible to company shipping.

41. The most likely cause of such a massive oil loss would be a war in which the Soviet Union (the only country with the naval strength required) succeeded in blocking all oil tanker shipments from the Persian Gulf. While this scenario seems no more improbable than those on which NATO spends its billions, it does portend a crisis of such magnitude that economies would be forced to decrease to whatever level of supply was available.

CHAPTER 8

1. This discussion is based on the author's *Oil and Security: Problems and Prospects of Importing Countries*, Adelphi Paper no. 136 (London: International Institute for Strategic Studies, 1977), pp. 5-7.

2. Several studies have concluded, however, that the "psychological" reaction to the curtailments of gasoline can have a substantial economic effect. For example, during the 1973-74 embargo, U.S. car sales declined sharply, apparently as a result of the consumer's fear of continuing gasoline shortages. However, more detailed studies reveal that while demand for large automobiles dropped sharply, the demand for compacts actually increased beyond the capability of companies to supply them. See U.S. Federal Energy Administration, *The Short-Term Microeconomic Impact of the Oil Embargo* (Washington, D.C.: Government Printing Office, n.d.).

3. See U.S. Federal Energy Administration, *Strategic Petroleum Reserve Plan* (Washington, D.C.: Government Printing Office, December 15, 1976), p. A-5; and

S. Tani and D. Boyd, *Measuring the Economic Cost of an Oil Embargo* (Menlo Park, Calif.: Stanford Research Institute, October 1976) (available at the National Technical Information Service, Washington, D.C.).

4. Federal Energy Administration, *Plan,* pp. 25-26.

5. Ibid., pp. 25-27.

6. Peter Kihss, "Jersey Utilities Face Coal Conservation Step in March," *New York Times,* February 16, 1978.

7. U.S. Congress, Senate, Committee on Interior and Insular Affairs, *Agreement on an International Energy Program* (Washington, D.C.: Government Printing Office, 1974), art. 20.

8. In fact, one of the most interesting aspects of a scenario in which all IEA countries draw down emergency reserves is how they will rebuild stocks afterward. If they all try to do so simultaneously, their collective demand for emergency supplies when the crisis "ends" could so strain OPEC capacity that the postcrisis market would remain "tight." In effect, demand for emergency stocks could cause a perpetuation of a "shortage," which would most likely prompt escalations in OPEC prices, etc.

9. It is necessary to convert the emergency reserve drawdown level from 2 percent of consumption to its net import equivalent. Since the IEA as a group imports about 60 percent of its supplies, this can be done by dividing 2 percent by 0.60, which yields 3.3 percent.

10. See pages 38-39. For a more extensive evaluation of the implications of targeted embargoes, see the author's *Oil and Security.*

11. For this analogy, thanks go to Dr. Harald Leuba of Washington, D.C. Dr. Leuba attempted to obtain information on strike fund management from several unions but without success.

12. Walter J. Levy, "A Warning to the Oil Importing Nations," *Fortune,* May 21, 1979, pp. 48-51.

CHAPTER 9

1. See the analysis by Dr. Egon Balas in U.S. Congress, Senate, Committee on Interior and Insular Affairs, *Hearings: Review of the Strategic Petroleum Reserve Plan* (Washington, D.C.: Government Printing Office, 1977), pp. 492-508.

2. For example, see pages 90-91.

APPENDIX

1. This is borne out by the relatively small changes in the level of product stocks that have occurred.

2. Alaskan oil production jumped from less than 200,000 b/d in May 1977 to more than 800,000 b/d in September 1977, and reached 1.3 million b/d in May 1978. U.S. Department of the Interior, Bureau of Mines, *Mineral Industry Surveys: Monthly Petroleum Statements* (Washington, D.C., May-September 1977), tables 3 and 7.

3. That is, if month-end stock data were available, the March 1977 low might have a much smaller impact (1 in 12 rather than 1 in 4) on the average presented in table A-1.

4. Organization for Economic Cooperation and Development, *Quarterly Oil Statistics* (Paris: OECD).

5. For further discussion of these assumptions, see pages 82-83.

6. National Petroleum Council, *Petroleum Storage Capacity* (Washington, D.C.: NPC, September 1974), p. 51.

7. Although in Japan 400,000 barrels of crude oil are burned directly each day.

8. Even within the 32-day figure, the government and the industry believe, there

exists some flexibility to meet Dutch needs. Thus the interim CSO plan allows companies to count up to 20 percent of their export stocks toward their Dutch obligations.

9. The publication can be obtained from the Documents Expediting Project, Exchange and Gifts Division, Library of Congress, Washington, D.C. 20540.

10. For a useful comparison of terms and technical specifications in Europe, see annex 2 of the European Economic Community's *Energy Statistics, 1970-74* (Brussels, 1975).

Index

•

169

The Johns Hopkins University Press
This book was composed in Compugraphic English Times text
and display type by Action Comp Co. Inc. It was printed and bound
by The Maple Press Company.